Once Upon a Time in

HEAVEN

TRACY D. PALMER

ISBN 978-1-64492-502-7 (paperback)
ISBN 978-1-64492-503-4 (digital)

Christian Faith Publishing, Inc.
832 Park Avenue
Meadville, PA 16335
www.christianfaithpublishing.com

Printed in the United States of America

This book is dedicated to my best friend and biggest fan, Cynthia Alexander, for always seeing my best when I couldn't find it with a magnifying glass; my daughter, Brittney Palmer Ortiz, for all her strength and maturity in making sure that my life was saved and for loving on me when I was asleep; my sister, Kim Palmer, for always being there and keeping it together when we all want to fall apart; my good friend Jhan Beaupre for setting me back on the road to finishing this book and for keeping me close to his heart; and last but never least, my granddaughter, Sofia Ortiz, for making me smile with her giggles, breaking my heart with her tears, and for calling me Love every day.

FOREWORD

I must admit that when Tracy approached me and asked me to write the foreword for her book, I had one of those warm, peaceful feelings that let me know that God had put us in each other's lives for a reason. As I began to read the book, I knew I was correct. Reading this book was truly a gift. It is not hard to see the divine inspiration in the words written in its pages. If you have ever wondered what heaven might really be like, reading this book will paint a vivid picture for you. The combination of personal and pop culture makes the book accessible to people of varied interests and backgrounds. The imagery is so real that you almost feel that you can reach out and touch the objects and people she describes. While this may be classified as a work of fiction, as a Christian, there is no denying the hand of God guiding Tracy to put these words to paper.

Growing up in a Christian home, Tracy's foundation was built from an early age; finding the perfect church home as a young adult helped build her personal relationship with God. Learning from the teachings of Pastor Bob Nichols at Calvary Cathedral in Fort Worth, Texas, and listening to visiting evangelists like Joyce Meyer, Reinhardt Bonnke, and Tim Storey helped build her knowledge of God's Word and his gifts. I can only imagine Tracy's feelings as she recognized that twice in eight days, it had been prophesied to her that she was "the writer of the vision." But one cannot deny that the experiences of her life came together to allow Tracy to have the faith necessary to simply allow these words to flow through her fingertips as she felt God's direction.

Reading her book was a truly eye-opening and mind-expanding experience for me. It's not just the streets of gold and the mansions of our dreams that we all should expect, but it's the feelings that the words strung together in this book evoke. The comforts of total acceptance and total belonging bring an inner joy that we seldom experience in our earthly life. When we move from this world to the next, why wouldn't we feel God, the Father, Son, and Holy Spirit hold us in his arms and welcome us home? I don't know how anyone could read the words in this book and not see them unfold right in front of their eyes. Surely there will be those that read Tracy's words and then question whether she or God was indeed the writer. I myself can't imagine why our Heavenly Father wouldn't want for us all to experience the wonderful things laid out in this book. Why wouldn't he want to give us a glimpse of what's to come? How could anyone be certain that God is not speaking to us through this delightful book?

As a Christian woman, I have been privileged to be involved over the years in several conversations having to do with the subject matter of God, heaven, and angels. While I know, of course, we all have our own opinions about what may lie ahead of us on the other side, I am often amazed by the vein of similarities in our visions, and this book certainly shares those themes. I am happy to have been asked to read this book and to write the foreword for it, and I hope it is read the world over. I believe it will make you smile, think, cry, and laugh. What's a good book without those things, anyway? I have the feeling that I will go back to this book time and time again to see what else God has for me in its pages. I think that is exactly what this work is supposed to do.

Leslie E. Boutcher, PhD

PREFACE

*O*nce Upon a Time in Heaven is written by a first-time novelist and inspired by God. This is a book that has been worked on over a number of years covering several subjects. What you will take from this work is totally dependent on the things you have learned from your own studies and God experiences. This book has been put to paper because years ago, God called me to be "the writer of the vision." I must believe that this work is that vision or is the initial step to it. The words you find in this book may not be your cup of tea or where you come from spiritually, but I don't believe that is the point of God's inspiration on it. I believe it simply has been given in this way for his reasons, and I do hope that you take from it what God has for you.

A month or so after I finished the book and prepared to upload it on Amazon, in a strange turn of events…I died. I had a sudden asthma attack and died in the ambulance on the way to the hospital with my pregnant daughter in tow. I was intubated, sent to ICU, and connected to machines that breathed for me. I was loaded with powerful medications that were said to be able to settle a three-hundred-pound sumo wrestler, but my metabolism was so fast that my body simply drank them in without the desired effect. I guess I was not going silently into the night. I was restrained and remedicated to keep me from fighting the lifesaving equipment that had been placed down my throat. My family and friends stayed with me for the three days I lay in ICU. The removal of the tubes left me free to *talk*, and as per my family, boy did I. I was drugged out of my mind and free to speak. I attempted to give my mother the finger and to tell her, "This is for you." (It's good that she knew I was under heavy medication or I'm sure I would have remained in the hospital longer than originally necessary.) I asked my sister who'd flown in from Atlanta, "What are *you* doing here?" I am told that I put on the "cloak of truth" and told all my loved ones about themselves. In and out of consciousness, I lay for three days before being moved to a regular room in the hospital. I was told that I sexually harassed all the good-looking male nurses that had come in to care for me... Yeah, that sounds like me.

After waking in my new room, I opened my eyes to find my three-year-old cousin sitting with her parents at the end of my bed. After everything I had been through, that one sight let me know something was really wrong with this picture. As I woke and scanned the room, I saw my mother, cousins, and sisters and realized where I was but had no memory of how I got there or why. The missing pieces of my memory were filled in during the days that followed and mostly brought laughter; apparently under heavy medication, I am quite the comedian.

It seems that in situations like mine, God releases miracles, the first of which was sparing my life. But in addition to that, he poured out miracles and blessings on all those who came and gathered around me. I heard that there were deeper, more emotion-filled conversations among family and friends that had taken place while I slept than in several years of me being wide awake. There is always something deeper in how God works. He is always behind the scenes directing the traffic of our lives, and if we just slow down, listen, and open up, we may just wake up to what he has for us. Maybe this little book is God's way of providing literary medication so that we won't fight the lifesaving equipment he brings into our existence.

God is amazing! He is so amazing that our human, mortal minds can't truly grasp all that he is and can be to us if we just let go of our egos and our thoughts of unworthiness. I know that God wants us to soar and experience all that he has for us; he just requires that we find a way to do this in the physical covering of skin, flesh, and bone. I hope that you enjoy this work and are able to extract something just for you. I hope that it may comfort you in any time of need, especially if there has been a loss. I am hopeful that having a picture of where your loved one may be will give you the peace you seek.

Enjoy and God bless.

Tracy D. Palmer

CHAPTER 1

Sabbath Day

Once upon a time in heaven, a soul arrived, and it was mine. I don't know what ended my life on earth, but whatever it was, it seemed far from important now. I looked down to find myself clothed in an exquisite wrap dress. It was beautiful, white, and iridescent. The dress fell just above my knees, and with it, I wore three-inch white slingbacks. I was happy that the shoes didn't pinch and that they were as comfortable as my favorite slippers.

I began to walk down what appeared to be a dimly lit corridor and wondered if I was in the right place. I'd always heard people say, "Go toward the light!" Somehow I thought the light would be brighter. Something made me continue on. I was at peace, comfortable, and…not the least bit warm. That was a good sign.

As I continued my walk, I noticed double doors in the distance; there was a man standing there. I could not make out his face, but he beckoned me to come closer. Still I felt comfort and at peace even as he began to give me the "hurry hand." I quickened my pace. As I arrived at the doors, I looked up into the face of my grandfather Russell Preuitt, Bum as we used to call him. He looked so wonderful to me. Though he had passed on years before, he looked just as I remembered.

His arms opened and enveloped me like a warm, familiar blanket. "Welcome home, sweetie," he said.

As I closed my eyes and took in the experience, the flood of loving memories made me smile. It felt like heaven. It felt like home. I had not seen Bum for several years prior to his death. He and Grandmother lived in Bakersfield, but seeing him now was like it was just yesterday. I smiled up at him, and he, down at me.

As his arms opened up to release me, the walls and doors of the long corridor began to fade away, and the brightest light encircled the two of us. It was the brightest light I had ever seen, but somehow it did not make me squint.

Bum stepped aside to allow me to see what lay ahead. It was more astonishing than any words could express. The sun shone brightly, but I could not see it anywhere. Everywhere I looked, I was more amazed. The descriptions I'd heard of what heaven looked like were true and so much more; there were people and animals everywhere. The streets of gold and the precious jewels were all here. As we began to walk, my nostrils were filled with the fragrance of the air; it was sweet but unlike anything I'd ever smelled before. Bum gave me the grand tour. As he walked, I noticed there was pep in his step; he strolled through this place like an excited teenager. He showed me the walls of jasper that surrounded the city, the river of life, and the tree of life with all its fruit. I watched as both people and animals pulled from the tree; some gathered the fruit in beautifully woven baskets, and still others simply ate it as they stood covered by its graceful branches. Bum and I sat on the bank of the river at the base of the tree made famous by the words written in God's Word. The river was crystal clear, and the fruit sparkled like multicolored diamonds. We chatted a bit before moving on.

Bum showed me the field where he said five of the disciples held classes. Then we spotted them. They were just beginning to set up as we passed. My grandfather waved his hand and yelled out, "Hey, fellas, how's it going?"

Mark yelled back, "All is well! We are blessed of the Lord!" Then he said, "Welcome home, Tracy." I coyly smiled and waved in his direction—it was *Mark*. I was stunned that he knew me! A chorus of greetings split the air.

"Good to see you, Tracy!"

"Welcome!"

"Glad you made it!"

Matthew, Mark, Luke, John, and Peter knew me! It was as if I were meeting the Jackson Five back in 1974. They were magnificent. There, twenty feet in front of me they stood, those who had walked and talked with Jesus as he started his ministry on earth. They were friends who shared food, drink, conversation, and laughter with the Lord. I was in awe. As my mouth hung open, Bum stepped in front of me with his hands on his hips and asked, "What are you doing?"

"What do you mean?" was my response. "It's them," the words left my mouth in a whisper, "the *disciples!*" I was as giddy as a schoolgirl.

"The Father," Bum went on, "is no respecter of persons. He called them just like he did you and me. Pick up your lip and come on."

My grandfather did not mince words. "Okay, I had a momentary lapse. I'm new here," I said. With a smile creasing just the corner of his lips expressing his delight, Bum continued to walk. He told me about things that had happened in my life as I was growing up—things that I knew neither he nor my grandmother was present to have witnessed.

He told me how proud he had always been of me. As he spoke those words to me, I realized that we had stopped walking. He turned and said, "Well, here we are." I turned and noticed that we had stopped in front of a gigantic open-air stadium.

The Jesus Concert, Live!

From the large structure, I could hear music and clapping, laughter, and singing. As I walked through the shadows of the cavernous passageway into the stadium, I realized I was no longer in the presence of my grandfather, but I knew somehow that he was still with me. We were still connected—I could just feel it.

I stepped onto the floor of the stadium and stood at the back of what felt like hundreds of thousands of people. They were of all races, all ages. There were men and women, young girls and boys. Then I noticed their clothing. There were people that appeared to be from all periods. There were people wearing animal skins and feathered headdresses. I saw pilgrims, flapper girls, Civil War soldiers, 1940s sailors, and I think I saw Amelia Earhart. I saw little girls and boys clapping and singing and dancing. The sight was bigger than anything I'd ever seen.

At the front of this large crowd was a platform, and on it…there *he* was. I'd know him anywhere. He looked like me, like us. He was singing and clapping his hands in worship to his father. As I tilted my head to get a better view of him, I noticed that he too tilted his head. I was taken aback. It almost looked as if he was looking at *me*. But that just couldn't be. There were thousands upon thousands of people between him and me; he could not have noticed me.

I was amazed that I seemed to instantly know what was being sung as if I'd been singing it for years. Singing the songs delighted and encouraged me. My foot began to tap, and I clapped along with the music. I spun to the left and then to the right; I swayed back and forth as I sang. My whole body was filled with praise. I slowed my rhythm to just take in the fullness of what I was seeing.

I looked toward my Savior again and saw that he now stood still as the group continued to explode in praise. His eyes caught mine. He was looking at me. Me—I couldn't believe it. As the crowd swayed and moved, he tilted his head once more to keep the eye contact. He smiled and did something that brought me to my knees. He, Christ Jesus, Son of Almighty God, with a smile, lifted his right hand and waved at me!

I could feel all the strength drain from my legs as I dropped to my knees on the stadium floor. Now all I could see was the palms of my own two hands. I could hardly breathe; I couldn't stop the tears from flowing. I could faintly hear myself repeating the words "I am not worthy." Instantly, all fell silent; the immediate removal of sound was jarring and exciting all at the same time.

I lifted my head from my hands to see that the enormous crowd was gone. There was no music, no singing, and no clapping. There was just him and me. The distance between us was a football field, but instead of standing on the platform, he stood on the field as I did. Although the distance was great, I could see him clearly.

Every fiber of my being said, "Run." I took off in the direction of my Savior. I ran what seemed to be three steps before he scooped me into his arms like I was a newborn baby. I cried as he spoke to me. I cried as he said those words that every believer wants to hear.

"Well done, Tracy, and...welcome home."

In his arms, so many things became clear; so many questions were answered without a word being spoken. As I lay there in his arms I realized that all this time, I had been *realizing* things—just as I did on earth. *That can't be right*, I thought. *Shouldn't I have a new frame of mind? Shouldn't everything be new and unfamiliar?*

I lifted my face, full of questions, but looking into his eyes, I had all the answers. Would my earthly parents strip me of all I knew, of all their love in an instant and leave me with strangers and expect for it not to faze or frighten me? Would my earthly parents take away the essence of which I am, the one they say they love? Why would God, the perfect, loving parent, want to change me into someone or something else when it was he who created me in the first place?

As understanding poured into me, I was no longer in the arms of my Lord but walking beside him on the glistening street. This street led into what I could only describe as a neighborhood, a very different neighborhood. What I saw was expansive, like a huge city, but it felt like a cul-de-sac where everyone knew one another. There was music, whisper soft that felt like praise and glory and worship. I noticed as I walked that Jesus was no longer beside me but about fifty yards ahead and was seated with someone on a bench. They were talking. I was amazed that I could still feel him right next to me. I thought, *This is going to be good. It's all win-win here! No evil, no spite, no harm.* Here there was only good, only love, only peace.

CHAPTER 2

James, the Other One

I began to walk toward the bench where Jesus sat. I noticed everything around me was pristine, but it looked effortless for it to be that way. There were no trash cans or sewer drains, no power lines or water towers. It was the way God had always intended it to be, but we, man had our own ideas. We leaned on our own understanding, and we fell. We fell from grace. We fell from the peace and pristine that is this place. From then on, the plan was to get us back here, back home where he is. I knew that now, standing in this place.

I stepped off the street and onto the grass. I noticed, as I could not help but look down, that the grass sparkled. Not only did it sparkle; it swayed. Not only did it sway; it sang. I was delighted but frozen, as I did not want to hurt it or crush it beneath my feet.

"Please," the blades of grass spoke in unison, "do not concern yourself. We would be honored to have you walk upon us."

"Thank you," I said, "but you are so beautiful."

"Our beauty is in the Lord. We honor him as we honor you. Welcome home." The grass continued to sing, sway, and sparkle as I came closer to the bench where Jesus and his friend sat.

Approaching the man whose back was to me, I felt familiarity, comfort, and expectation. I would not normally interrupt, but I felt "called." As I neared him, he stood. I recognized him even before he faced me. It was James, the first real love of my life. At that moment, I still didn't remember my death, but I remembered his.

I remembered the day, the collapse, and the ambulance. I remembered the hallway of the emergency room becoming longer with every step as the hallway did for Jobeth, Williams in the movie *Poltergeist*. In thinking about it, I felt no pain or sorrow; I simply remembered it as I would remember a story I'd read in a magazine. As with my grandfather, it was as if it were only yesterday that we'd seen each other. James smiled at me.

"Hello, Tracy. You look like heaven."

"So do you," I said with ease and a smile.

"Please sit," he said, offering me a place on the bench. I noticed then that I no longer saw Jesus on the bench, but I could feel him everywhere.

James and I sat and looked out into heaven. The sky was lit up with colors, some I'd seen before, some I had not. Just then, the colors were replaced by sound and images. It was like being at the largest drive-in movie ever. The images spanned the sky and space all around us. The "movie" was showing some of the world's history, the *actual* history in real images.

Before me, I saw the Father create and breathe life into Adam and then take a rib from his sleeping body to create Eve. As they both awoke and saw each other for the first time, they were pleased. They both had dark skin and hair; Eve's hair flowed past her hips, and she made Adam smile for the first time. I saw their love for each other and for their Creator.

I saw God walk with them, speak with them, and minister to them. He taught them about the garden and about himself. Every day, man's relationship with the Father grew.

The garden was more beautiful than I could ever have imagined; the plants were exotic and fragrant, and they bloomed everywhere. The first two humans explored the garden and each other. They spoke the first language, which I could somehow understand as I stood in their midst. I saw the serpent as he set his sights on the woman and how he'd begun to spin his web of lies and deceit as she, at times, walked alone in her new home. Eve was more beautiful than any woman I had ever seen in my lifetime, but why wouldn't she be? She was the first woman; she was the mold for us all. She was as perfect as a woman could be; her eyes were beautiful and dark, her hair was long and manageable, and her skin was the color of deep copper. Her gait as she walked was elegant, and I could hear her humming as she walked through her home. I was awed by the woman that stood just ten feet from me in this beautiful place.

I saw how Eve was taken in and overpowered by the serpent's words. She was not the stupid, ridiculous woman humanity had thought she'd been throughout history. She was a woman seduced into making a bad decision.

Being seduced by Satan in person was so much different from just struggling with right and wrong. This seduction was real, and she was face-to-face with it. In that moment, her husband was not with her to help her stand on her faith. She was alone in this beautiful place with this beautiful tree with this serpent that spoke to her in such a smooth, calming tone. It was as if the seduction were set to music. It lulled her into a false sense of security that was deep and intoxicating.

As I watched the images play out in front of me, I wept for her—and for all the judgments I had made about her over the span of my life before coming to the Lord. *If it hadn't been for Eve's decision, my life would have been perfect*, I had often shamelessly thought.

Swayed

I saw the image of Eve presenting the idea to her husband. He resisted at first, but he loved her. She swayed him just like so many of us sway our modern-day husbands into doing some crazy things, because they love us. My tears flowed as they each took a bite and instantly realized what they should not have known. I could feel myself saying no at the image and James tugging on my arm like you would an overly zealous date who thought telling the girl in the movie "Don't go in there" would somehow save her life.

I watched as they realized their nakedness and their shame. I could see the realization on their faces that the life they had just moments ago was gone. The images played on all around us as if we too were there in that garden. It was so real and emotional. Although James had seen the same images upon his arrival, I could see that they still affected him as deeply as they did me.

I could feel the guilt and shame as Eve and Adam ran and hid from the Father as he searched for them. What they had done could not be reversed, and they were not only sorry for what they had done, but they feared seeing the disappointment and betrayal in the eyes of their Father.

The Father found the two huddled together at the base of a tree; the serpent could be seen in its branches. Adam covered his wife, and she held on to him.

"Adam, why do you hide yourselves from me?" the Father asked.

"We were naked and ashamed," Adam barely whispered.

"How do you know that you are naked?"

"We ate of the tree that you told us not to eat. The serpent seduced the woman, she ate, and…I followed."

I could see the Father's hurt, disappointment, and anger. His eyes narrowed as he reached for the serpent. The serpent reared back and growled as if to threaten God. In an instant, the Father grabbed the serpent about the neck and gave a little squeeze as he brought him closer to his face.

"Because you have done this thing," God said, "you are cursed. You will slink along the earth on your belly for the rest of your life."

My breath caught as I saw the body of the serpent begin to change. I could hear his screams and the sound of his bones breaking as the metamorphosis took place. A glow could be seen from the Father's hand as he held the serpent's throat and the beast took its new form.

"You will forever be at war with the woman and her offspring. She will wound your head, and you, her heel." The Father then threw the serpent from the garden with one toss. God's new creation lay there, dazed and in pain. He did not know what to do without the legs he'd been accustomed to. It was then Eve's turn.

"Woman," God said, "I will multiply your pain in childbirth. What should be most beautiful will henceforth be most painful. You will want to please your husband, but it will seem impossible. What you have done, woman, will bring pain and repercussions for all the seed of man." Eve lowered her head and wept.

"And, Adam," the Father continued, turning a glaring eye onto the man, "because you have been led by your wife and you did eat of the tree, the very ground you were formed from shall be cursed. The ground from which you will get food will rebel against you. The pain your wife feels in childbirth you will feel in coaxing food from the ground. It will require backbreaking work to feed your family. You will work in pain your whole life long, and when your life has ended, you will return to the dust."

As I watched the sentencing, I could see the pain in all their eyes. This was a horrible situation for them all. The Father closed the garden to them and set a guard at its gates. He provided clothing for them from animal skins and set them to work the ground from which they came. As the Father turned and walked back through the garden, I could see him weeping; his heart was broken. As he walked past the tree, it disappeared. I knew it had been replanted in the kingdom of heaven.

Adam and his wife set out into the wilderness that had now become their home. They could not blame the Father; they could only be grateful that they still drew breath. Adam told his wife that they would, from that moment, do everything to please their Creator. Eve agreed.

CHAPTER 3

Home Sweet Home

The next images seemed to play in fast motion. I took in so much information in what seemed like seconds, and then the images were gone and replaced by the beautiful colors I'd seen earlier. I knew there would be more for me to see and learn at a later time. Although I'd seen such heart-wrenching and emotional images, I now felt no pain or sadness; I was at peace.

"Thank you," James said.

"For what?" I asked.

"Thank you for taking on my responsibility when I had to leave."

"It was God's plan that the girls remain with me," I said. "I had no choice."

"You did have a choice, so thank you."

I responded with a smile and a nod of "You're welcome."

"Come with me," he said.

We walked on the grass as it sang praises to the Lord. We passed mansions on either side of the street. Their occupants all stood outside, waving and welcoming me. There was Diana, Princess of Wales, Coretta Scott King, and Mother Teresa. I knew she'd be here. They all greeted me with smiles and hugs as if we'd all grown up together.

James walked me farther down the street, where we stopped in front of a beautiful French château. As I stood there taking in its grandeur, the stained glass windows and stone facade, I knew it was mine. It was the mansion God himself prepared for me.

As I looked over at James, he smiled. He extended his hand to help me with my jaw that had fallen open.

"So this is it," he said.

"What do you mean?" I asked.

"This is the desire of your heart."

I turned to look at it once more. "Yes, I guess it is."

"Well, I'll see you again," he said.

"Aren't you coming in?"

"No, this is the desire of your heart. Besides, you have visitors."

My eyes took in this man that I had loved. I remembered how he had helped soothe and comfort and rebuild my heart after it had been so broken in my marriage.

We spoke a minute more, and then he was gone. I knew somehow that when I wanted to see him again, I would. My eyes took it all in. When Jesus said, "In my Father's house, there are many mansions," he wasn't kidding. All around me were those mansions. Still my neighbors were waving, smiling, and welcoming me. I had never felt so welcome anywhere, but I guess if you want to feel welcome, this is the place to be. I waved at my neighbors and headed up the stairs to my front doors.

Upon reaching the top of the stairs, I noticed that on either side of the entrance stood a magnificent angel. I always wanted two large angels to flank the entrance of my dream home. When God does a thing, he does a good thing. As I stood in front of the doors between the two angels, I noticed that they were real, live angels. I was stunned.

"Welcome home. I am Merkin," the angel spoke. "I will stand on the right."

"And I," the other said, "am Chezen. I will stand on the left."

"Hello," I said. "Are you my visitors?"

"No," Merkin said, "we are the desire of your heart."

"I don't understand," I said. "I'm new here."

"Is it not the desire of your heart to live in a French château and have your front doors flanked by angels?" Chezen asked.

"Well, yes," I replied. "But I was thinking maybe stone or marble, you two are alive."

"Yes, we are," they spoke in unison.

"Are you saying that it is your job to stand on either side of my front doors?" I questioned.

"No," Merkin answered. "We *are* your front doors."

Their voices permeated my spirit. I took a step back to really appreciate what I was seeing. There before me stood two huge living, breathing angels. They stood about seven feet tall. Their skin was the color of bronze, dark and creamy. They were both muscular—not like the Incredible Hulk, but more like the actor turned California governor, in the early years when he hadn't yet gotten a firm grip on the English language.

They were dressed identically in beige-colored loincloths with leather banding at the waist. Leather strapped sandals were laced up their huge calves. They both had shoulder-length hair held back by a leather strap. Chezen's locks were blond, and Merkin's were a beautiful chocolate brown. Both held a shield and a spear, and in the shadow of their huge broad shoulders, I could see the hint of imposing wings tucked behind. I was impressed. The scope of the two was overwhelming. I was honored to have them stand for me. I smiled, and they bowed their heads to me. Merkin, Chezen, and I spoke for a few minutes more before my attention was turned to a small patch of landscaping to the right of the front doors. There were multicolored flowers that were illuminated—pink, purple, yellow, orange, and green; they all shone like multicolored glow sticks. They sang softly and swayed to the song being sung by the grass in my front yard.

I smiled in amazement with what my eyes and ears beheld. To the left of the doors was an opulent settee overstuffed and loaded with comfy pillows; it looked so inviting. I, not being one to turn down an invitation, was drawn closer. As I reclined upon the settee, it enveloped me, and I felt warmth and comfort like a newborn baby swaddled in its mother's arms. I sank into the feeling, and my whole being felt so...*alive.*

I did not want to leave the comfort of the settee, but I remembered that I still had guests inside. As I walked away, I looked back and knew that if a piece of outdoor furniture could make me feel like that, I had much more in store for me in the wonderful place.

Visitors Revealed

I entered my new home. As I stood just inside, I knew for the first time *ever* that I was a no-mortgage, no-phone, no-light-bill homeowner. It was all mine, and it felt like me, like I had always been there. Every room I stepped into was decorated the way I would have done it myself. Everything was comfortable and made from the finest materials. As I walked into what seemed like the great room, the smell of fresh flowers flooded the room. I noticed the piano. It was wonderful, black, and shiny. I remembered that I had never taken a piano lesson even though I had always hoped to.

As I walked over to admire the beautiful instrument, I fully expected to see the name Steinway, but instead, emblazoned on it was the name Jehovah. I was so honored, and I felt my eyes begin to tear. The thought of God crafting this instrument himself almost took my breath away. Just then, I thought back on my experiences since my arrival; something told me that if I sat down at that piano, I would be able to play anything that came to mind. The thought brought a smile to my face. I heard voices and remembered that I still had guests waiting. The voices led me to the kitchen.

As I walked in, I knew there was really no need to cook here, but the smell of steak and pancake syrup made me happy. I had the feeling that God included it because it was what I was used to, and besides, what's a French château without a kitchen? I looked to my left, and there they were, all three of them together in my home, in my kitchen, and...cooking, no less.

They all stood facing me as if royalty was receiving them. I could only lie myself out facedown on the perfectly tiled floor in an effort to show my humility. I could not get low enough before them. Father, Son, and Holy Ghost right there in my kitchen. I wept as I felt them come closer and gather round me. As I lay outstretched, I could feel my Father's hands as he grasped mine. He raised me to my feet and stood me in front of him, but I could not look at him. With his hand, he lifted my head and said, "Open your eyes, my child, and look upon your Father."

My eyes opened, and there he was, with Jesus and the Holy Spirit on either side; they smiled at me. They were all so glorious, almost too much to take in, but I was unable to look away. The feeling I had of being *alive* on my front porch was nothing compared to what I now felt as my hands lay in the hands of the Father. I felt *everything* from the light of this place to the smallest sparkling blade of grass and everything in between.

As they looked at me, I could feel their vision inside, outside, and all over me. There was such love in their eyes for me, as if I had been a lost child and now I had been found, as if they were waiting to show themselves to me. The three encircled me in a heavenly group hug. I could actually feel them all. The experience was better than anything I had ever felt. It was better than winning the lottery or getting a promotion. On earth, after the birth of my daughter, I thought those two things would feel the best.

When the holy hug ended, the Father began to speak.

"Hello, my child," he said in a voice so warm and comforting. It was like James Earl Jones, Morgan Freeman, and Sean Connery rolled into one, only so much better.

"Hello, Father," I said as I felt tears well up in my eyes. I thought about what I had said: "Father." It was always such a big word to me. I would never have called my earthly father by that title. I would use "Dad," "Daddy," or just plain "Lee Roy" when it fit the situation, but nothing so big and formal as the word "Father." As I stared into the face of God, I saw love—pure love, the kind of love that says, "You are the greatest thing since sliced bread, and you are the one I think of before I think of myself," the kind of love that says, "I would die so that you might live." It was the kind of love that melts you like wax.

He smiled at me and began to speak. I knew that what he was about to say would be so powerful that I would never forget it. As he opened his mouth, this is what he said: "How about a steak and egg omelet?"

"Ah…sure," I said.

"Sit down. Jesus will bring you some coffee, and then we'll talk over breakfast."

I couldn't believe what I was hearing or seeing. God the Father, creator of the universe, was cracking eggs in my kitchen. Just then, I noticed Jesus pouring coffee into my favorite mug, and he added the cream and sugar just as I like it. As the Son came closer to me, I felt his love and warmth. What a special time this was—Jesus preparing and bringing me a cup of coffee. After our time in the stadium, I wondered what amazing thing he would say to me. It all felt so surreal. It was like waking up on Thanksgiving morning and coming down to breakfast with the whole family. The Holy Spirit was mixing pancake batter, for goodness sake.

Jesus sat the cup down in front of me. As he sat in the chair next to me, he smiled—not a smile you'd expect from the Lord and Savior, but one you'd expect from your goofy older brother, a smile that made my left eyebrow go up in anticipation of what was to follow.

Jesus reached his hand out to me as if in slow motion to maybe, I thought, put it on my shoulder or to lightly rub my cheek. Nothing could have been further from the truth. The Lord God Almighty laid his hand on the top of my head and tousled my hair like I was a seven-year-old.

"I'll see you later, squirt," he said, and then he was gone.

I could still feel him, and the whole event made me giggle. The Father placed the omelet in front of me, and the Holy Spirit followed with the pancakes and syrup. As we began to eat the wonderful meal, the Father began to speak. "It is good that you are here. I am pleased that you made time for me in your life when you had the choice not to. I am pleased that you had faith in me. You had faith that I was always here," he said as he put another pancake on his plate.

"I couldn't help but feel you, Father, and see you in everything," I responded.

"Tracy, I have been with you always. Since your beginning, I've been with you. On the day of your birth, I stroked your hair as you lay in your mother's arms. She was so proud of you. I extended my finger to you as you took your first steps and helped you utter your first word. I was there for the good times…and, yes, for the bad ones as well."

The Father stood and moved toward the window and looked out. "I have always been watching you and laying out your path before you. Sometimes you strayed and made mistakes, but you always made your way back and learned the lesson. I've never wanted my people to be in pain, Tracy. I sometimes allow it so that my people learn and grow to help themselves and to help others. It works out well most of the time, but there are those who take the gift of free will and use it against me. They blame me for things that are not my doing and cry out to me for help in situations that their own free will had gotten them into. It saddens me that when I deliver them out of the situation, as they have asked, not only do they not thank me, they proceed to curse me. When they curse me, I bless them. I wake them each morning, I get them safely through the day, and I continue to watch over them. I love them, and still…they curse me," he said.

I could feel the Father's sadness. I could feel that he has wept for his people since the beginning.

"Walk with me, my child," he said.

As the Father, Holy Spirit, and I stepped out of the French château he'd built for me, I noticed the interaction at the entrance. "Merkin, Chezen," the Father said to my angels.

"We praise you, Father," they said as they bowed.

As they moved to make the gesture and their forms separated from the château, the château itself filled in the space left by their absence. As the angels each took one knee, the Father and the Holy Spirit placed a hand on each of their heads and blessed them. I saw a warm glow from the Father's hands as he held them in place. Merkin and Chezen rose as the two removed their hands. The angels stepped back and resumed their positions as the château made way.

"Tracy, I am always but a thought away," the Father said as he left my presence.

I stood between the angels as they departed. "He is magnificent," I said.

"Yes," they both agreed.

CHAPTER 4

A Girl's Best Friend

I went back into the château to explore. It really was grand. Everything I could ever imagine having in my home was there. Exquisite furnishings and oriental carpets, silk drapes, crystal, fresh flowers, and hardwood floors filled every inch. I walked toward the piano that I was now eager to play. Beethoven and Alicia Keys were going to get a run for their money.

As I neared the bench, I looked out into the manicured large garden and noticed a doghouse.

"No way," I said. I passed the lacquered piano bench and headed outside. "Mokie?" I called tentatively but with full expectation of seeing her, and out she sprang as if I just willed her into existence.

Jamocha Almond Fudge was her full AKC registered name. My mother had named her after her favorite ice cream. Mokie was a black-and-tan German shepherd. When I was a girl, she was my favorite "sister"; the two that I was born to didn't quite live up to my expectations. Mokie was my best friend. She kept all my secrets and heartaches, and she never told a soul. She slept in my bed, on my pillow, right next to me, although her breath left much to be desired. I loved her so much. I knew she'd be here. The day my mother took her on that "long ride" and she didn't come back with her was the day I prayed her into heaven.

I knew that God would give me the desires of my heart even then, and Mokie was definitely one of them. She jumped up to greet me as she always did. Mokie's presence was delightful; I had missed her so. I stroked her silky fur, and she thanked me by licking my face. I didn't normally like the saliva of dogs, but this was heaven; how bad could it be?

We played fetch in the garden for what seemed like hours. My friend later followed me into the house, and she stayed close to me wherever I went. After getting reacquainted with my old friend, I needed to see him, the one I'd cried over for so long. I knew that when I got here, I'd need to see him, and I knew exactly where he'd be: right next door. It was a desire of my heart, and all my desires seemed to be coming to pass in this place, so I didn't doubt it for a moment. I left the château and began the short walk next door. As I walked, I saw ahead of me a little girl playing with a jump rope. She wore pink footie pajamas and a tiara. As I came closer to her, she stopped to say hello and to welcome me. She extended to me her hand, and I took it. "Hello," she said, "my name is JonBenét."

"I know," I said.

"I am honored to meet you."

"I'm sorry to have disturbed your jump roping," I continued.

"Oh, you didn't," she said. "I have been playing here since I arrived, and I'm having the best time. I saw Jesus earlier, and he always makes me smile."

"Me too," I agreed.

Her hair was like spun gold, and her face was sweet and inno-cent; she smelled like cotton candy.

"I have to go, but I'll see you later, if that would be okay," I said.

"Yes," JonBenét replied, "maybe we could play a game or something."

"Sure, that would be great," I said.

"You'd better hurry," she said as I began to walk away. "He has been so eager since you arrived—you're a desire of his heart."

I left her with a smile on my face. I was so excited to see him. I approached the large home; it was as over the top as I thought it would be. I noticed a pit bull and a panda playing on the lawn. As I came closer to the entrance, I could hear music—not just any music, but rap music. This was not rap music that would make me want to pull my hair out; it was good stuff. I knew it was created for God by a musical genius—no, not Michael Jackson; be serious! I knocked on the large door; it opened, and there he was. My nephew, Christopher Palmer, had been murdered before his twenty-first birthday. He had just begun his business—Foundation Entertainment. His death was crushing to our family, and the Holy Spirit was called on often to bring peace to the situation. For years, on so many occasions after his death, I'd find myself just bursting into tears because he was gone from my life.

We were aunt and nephew, but we were so much more. We were friends and confidants. And here he stood in front of me, so full of life. I grabbed him close to me and held him tight. He was whole and healthy and absolutely fine; his presence filled my arms. After I released him, he flashed me one of those million-dollar smiles and welcomed me into the mansion God had built for him.

The home I stood in seemed to fit this young man perfectly. There were dark wooden pieces all around and big leather couches. The floors in the space were hardwood and covered in some places by exotic carpets. The back wall was made of windows, and light flooded the room. I was impressed; back on earth, his good furniture choices could fill a small brown paper bag. I had missed this young man so much, and here he stood in front of me, giving me the grand tour of his spectacular home. Just then, I realized that I had misjudged him. He was not the misguided, immature boy I thought I knew; he was a brilliant, deep-thinking soul who simply did not have the time to show me what he was really made of. How wondrous it is that the Father set heaven up so that the ones we lost are right at our fingertips.

Beautiful Music

I followed Christopher to his music studio, where he had created amazingly beautiful music for each member of the Trinity. I noticed that Father, Son, and Holy Ghost each had their own huge file of Chris Palmer creations. The music he created was not only his rap for God, but there were also songs of praise and worship and songs waiting to be given to artists on earth. I realized just then that the praise I heard being sung by the grass was one of his creations. "It's so good to see you," I told him.

"You too. I knew you'd be here before the others," he said.

"Did Bum greet you in the corridor when you arrived?" I asked.

"No, I've spent time with him since I arrived, but I was greeted by my fourth-grade soccer coach, Mr. Tucker. I knew him right away. I think it works that way. God presents to us someone from our past that we knew well and would be comforting to us. I had not had a relationship with Bum, so Mr. Tucker, someone I trusted and respected, greeted me."

Christopher and I talked further about each of our experiences here in heaven. He asked me how many "movies" I'd seen. I told him I had only the one session, and he told me that there was more to come. I told Christopher that I didn't remember my own death, but I remembered James's.

"Is that the way it's supposed to be?" I questioned.

"I think so," he said. "I have just recently been able to revisit what happened to me."

I only thought for half a second about asking him to tell me the tale, but even though I knew from experience that after hearing it, I would not feel pain, only peace, I could not ask him. I left Christopher after what seemed like forever. We talked and laughed about so many things. He told me of his experience here and of all those he met along the way. He told me of the garden he happened upon soon after his arrival; he spoke of its beauty as if he were a poet. I thought I saw a tear form in the corner of his eye as he spoke of it. If a garden was so beautiful that it made him wax so poetic and want to cry, that was a garden I had to see for myself. I would make it a point to find my way there. On my way home, I was so excited and expectant about the things to come; I knew that my experiences would not mirror Christopher's exactly, but I was ready to be thrilled.

As I began to walk toward the château, the singing, shining, swaying grass replaced the street and sidewalks. I looked out onto an expanse of grass the size of Central Park, the sky showing its magnificent colors. I started to walk, as I knew I should. I could hear the praise and worship the blades of grass sang, and it caused me to close my eyes, kneel, and lift my hands. I could feel the comforting breeze on the tips of my fingers. The feeling of giving everything in worship was all-encompassing; tears began to flow. I was so grateful to be in this place. Just then, my eyes opened, and there in front of me stood…Marilyn Monroe. I couldn't believe my eyes. She was just as beautiful as she had been in all the movies and photos I had seen. Every hair was in place, and her skin was flawless; she looked like live porcelain. "Hello, Tracy," she said. "I guess you did not expect to see me here."

I stood, and we began to walk together as I replied, "No, I'm sorry, I guess I didn't. The world was told that you committed suicide, and how could you be here after taking your own life? I suppose I'm stuck on that whole 'Thou Shall Not Kill' thing."

Marilyn smiled and began to take a seat on the grass; I followed as the blades bowed to receive us. We lay back in the grass like Gwyneth Paltrow in an Estee Lauder commercial. As she began to speak, colors, sounds, and images illuminated the sky. There were images of those in my natural mind that I would not have thought I'd ever see here: Rick James, Jimmy Hoffa, my fourth-grade teacher, Mr. Pinkus, and Marilyn herself. The images reflected each of the individual lives, further solidifying my earlier thought pattern. Just then, to my surprise, I saw the last moments of their lives.

What should be so personal and private was opened to my eyes. I saw them all; whether they were on their knees, in bed, or in a ball on the floor, they all spoke the same words: "Father, forgive me."

They all spoke to the Father in their last moments as if he were seated right next to them. God being so sweet, precious, and merciful allowed these three to express themselves to him before their final breath.

"You see, Tracy," Marilyn said, "while people may think they know the truth about a person or a situation, it's very possible that they are very, very wrong. A person's personal relationship with God is just that…personal."

I was allowed to see what really happened to them all. Rick James's death was pretty much how the media portrayed it, but it was a horrible accident. Here on the grass next to Marilyn, I saw what really happened to Jimmy Hoffa and where his remains are buried. Geraldo Rivera wasn't even close. I saw what actually happened in Marilyn's home that night; she did not die as we had been led to believe. The beautiful woman who lay next to me in the grass did not die by her own hand. As I witnessed the events, I turned to tell her how sorry I was for any derogatory thought I might have had about how I'd heard that she'd taken her own life. She looked at me with a smile of thanks, and with that, Marilyn was gone. In those moments, I realized how personal our relationship with God is truly supposed to be. In an instant, I found myself back on the sidewalk with Mokie. The movies presented to me seemed to be very "hit-and-run." *I'd have to get used to that,* I thought.

CHAPTER 5

Has Heaven Always Been Like This?

As I was walking back to the château, the sights and sounds were mind-blowing. Everything that I could see was in praise and honor of the Trinity. Father, Son, and Holy Ghost were being praised every second. A child riding his bike was in praise. The angels flying above were flying in praise. It was all so amazing; I was overwhelmed with it all. Just then, I realized that Mokie and I were no longer on the way home but on a grassy mountain overlooking a valley where a beautiful river flowed. As we sat on the grass, I noticed all the beautiful flowers. It was magnificently peaceful in this place. *It is as if it were created just for me,* I thought.

"It was," came the voice of the Father. I turned to find that he sat right next to me on the mountain.

"Has heaven always been like this?" I asked.

"No. Heaven has always been here, but it has been my children's hopes, dreams, and desires that make it what it is. You made this," he said as he panned his hand across the landscape that stretched before me.

"No way," I said.

"Way!" the Father responded.

As I looked out over the valley, I saw a colorful monarch butterfly flying toward us. Since my arrival here, I had not seen any insects.

34

No ants, flies, or bumblebees, but here, now, was a butterfly. As it came closer, it fluttered around me. It flew from me to the Father, and I noticed that it stopped midair in front of him and *bowed!* The Father nodded his head in acknowledgment, and the butterfly resumed her flight. The tiny creature put on a performance like I'd never seen before. The butterfly flew through the air with ease and precision; it was nothing less than glorious. There were spins and dives that flowed with the music and song of the grass. After the performance, the tiny butterfly landed on my left index finger.

"That was wonderful," I said to the splendid entertainer.

"Thank you. It's an honor to praise the Father."

"You are so right," I said.

The tiny performer, who introduced herself as Maxine, flew from my finger to the Father. I noticed that they began an animated conversation like long-lost friends. The Father listened intently and laughed at just the right times; the two were just delightful. Before leaving, Maxine placed a tiny kiss upon God's cheek, and with that, she flew away. I turned to the Father; he had been so kind to me, so loving and gentle. As I looked into his eyes, I felt his love and his warmth. I positioned myself in front of him, and while on my knees, I worshipped and praised him. It was more intense than any other praise and worship I had ever given. Tears flowed; my mind overflowed with all his goodness. I lifted my hands and sang to him. I stood and danced and clapped my hands before him. I was overcome. As I danced, sang, and clapped, I noticed that he did too. There we were together on the mountain that my heart's desire created, worshipping together. God inhabits the praises of his people. The Father left me after our impromptu praise session, and I began to explore the mountain and the valley I created in this most amazing place.

As I got to the valley floor, I noticed that wildflowers spread as far as my eyes could see. There were so many colors, and the scent was enthralling. As I walked a little further, a cabin appeared in front of me. There were trees everywhere; the smell of pine filled the air. A magnificent oak tree stood out front and to the right of the front door, and from a sturdy branch, a swing hung from two chains. The cabin had a wraparound porch and blue shutters; smoke billowed from the chimney. Climbing the stairs, I was eager to open the door. Upon crossing the threshold, I was enveloped by the delicious feel of home and freshly baked cookies. This cabin that I had never seen before felt like I'd always been here.

I looked toward the fireplace to find it lit up with a crackling, glowing fire. I took a seat in one of the overstuffed chairs next to the fire. After adjusting myself in the chair, I was more comfortable than I could ever remember being. Scanning the room, I noticed that just as in the château, it was decorated as I would have done it myself.

It's just perfect, I thought.

"It's just the way he planned it," the archangel Gabriel said as he appeared in the chair opposite of me. "It's exactly what you need it to be," he said with a smile.

"But why? How is this possible?" I returned.

He arose from the comfy chair to stand in front of me; he knelt before me and took my hands in his. He went on to tell me that every corner of heaven was created by its inhabitants, by the desires in the hearts of those on their way. Heaven is in constant creation. This creation factor is something that has always been a part of both heaven and earth, but man's self-imposed limitations and ego keep him from accessing it. It was so easy to understand what was being said, being so open in that moment. I knew that there was so much more to come and to learn in this place. The archangel and I parted ways, and as I began to walk home, I was more amazed by my surroundings— surroundings I myself created with just a fleeting thought.

Ehren

In front of the château, I stood there a moment with my four-legged friend, and as we looked in each other's eyes, Mokie spoke to me. "I've missed you," she said with her big brown eyes.

"And I, you" was my reply.

"Thank you for praying me into this place."

I smiled and touched the silky fur on her head and said, "It wouldn't have been the same without you." As I began to walk toward the house, Mokie walked with me. We stopped and sat on the step just outside the front doors, with Merkin and Chezen standing by. I watched the colors, listened to the music that lifted through the air, and watched JonBenét as she played with several other children that had joined her. Children—they were everywhere. I saw those who had died in childbirth or in accidents, children who had been aborted or died early from sickness or malnutrition. I soon realized that every child who had died since the beginning of time was here in this place and they were still children. Those children who had died at birth or before seemed to be about six years old. They were all content and happy. I began to think on things, and then I turned to find myself face-to-face with my Savior.

"There she is," he said, "in the blue dress. I was there with you, you know, as was Ehren. He stood guard outside the door."

"Yes, I suppose I knew," I said. "But I was so embarrassed and ashamed I could not acknowledge you. It was not what I wanted."

"I know," he said as he put his arm around me and allowed me to rest my head on his shoulder.

Even in discussing one of the lowest points in my life, here I felt only peace. Looking at her, I felt only peace. Watching her and the other children play made me smile. She was so pretty and tiny. She had a lovely smile and one dimple just like mine. After that terrible decision and that terrible day, I knew she'd be here.

I'd always thought I'd have some explaining to do, telling her how I was so young and I had nothing with which to support a baby and I should have been more careful so that none of this had happened. I was prepared to tell her that I had loved her even though I had done that terrible thing. Sitting next to Jesus on the steps and looking out at her, I knew that none of that mattered.

"This is a wonderful place," I told him.

"I like it too," he said. Jesus suggested that we walk, and I agreed to the idea. I felt like I'd never walked so much in my life on earth. But here, I thought, I'll never tire of it. I noticed that there was no heavenly public transportation, no cars or motorcycles. There were bicycles and tricycles, but only for the enjoyment of the children.

Everyone walked to their destination or simply arrived, every-one but…them. As Jesus and I walked, I noticed the shadow of flight above me. I was amazed yet again by what my eyes beheld. Over my head, there they flew—angels. They were huge and bigger than life. They looked just as I thought they would. They were magnificent. Their chests were massive, and their legs were chiseled and as big as tree trunks. Each of them had a wingspan of at least twelve feet. They were dressed sparingly with a loincloth, belted at the waist, and leather sandals that laced up the calf. Some had short hair; others had long.

There were males and females. Some held swords, and others, spears and shields. I was again in awe. I noticed that Jesus no longer stood with me, but of course, I still felt him. I couldn't take my eyes off them. They flew with the ease of majestic eagles. I couldn't keep from smiling. I stood in awe of them even as a shadow landed upon my whole being; I looked up, and there he stood in front of me. My spirit knew him immediately. It was Ehren, my guardian.

He had been there with me from the beginning. He walked before me when I took a wrong step, when I was where I should not have been. He rode on top of the car when I learned to drive and, from then on, kept me safe and covered those who rode with me. He's fought and won so many battles to keep me safe when the forces of my own choices attempted to end my life.

I smiled at the one who had been with me always as we began to walk. No introductions needed to be made. I knew him, and he knew me. Ehren and I walked down what I now knew was Angel's Row. There were thousands upon thousands of them, some flying through the air, while others sat talking with those who had been their charges. Still others gathered together, discussing something that seemed quite urgent.

"Am I keeping you from something important? Should you be involved in that discussion?" I asked.

"I am involved. Can you not see with whom they speak?" he said with a smile.

As he said the words, I looked over at the gathering of angels to find Ehren standing in the midst of them while simultaneously sitting next to me on a bench we'd just laid claim to. Viewing this phenomenon anywhere else would have caused me to lose my mind, but here it seemed to be business as usual.

"Is everything all right?" I asked.

"All is as it must be," he said. Ehren changed the subject as he began to speak about the night my cousin Lori and I were chased by a truck filled with five men.

"That was a scary situation for two young girls walking home from a softball game," he spoke.

I remembered the events of that night vividly—Lori and I both running like jackrabbits when we heard the tires screeching and the truck beginning to move in reverse. We were chased for two blocks until Lori knocked on a stranger's door, hoping to find a Good Samaritan. Ehren was there, covering me as I had ducked into some nearby bushes. I could hear the exchange among Lori, the Samaritan, and the truckload of scary men. The Samaritan was just that, and he quickly convinced the pursuers to move on. I realized as Ehren brought the experience back to my remembrance that Lori's angel was on duty that night as well. Ehren took me through so many instances of coverage during my life, right up until the Father called him from duty and, shortly thereafter, I entered the long corridor where I was met by my grandfather. The revelations I was being given in this place were, in a word, cool. The way things were given to me so vivid and with such love, I could barely contain myself.

"Tracy," Ehren said, "it is good to have you here. I have wanted to show my true self to you for so long. The Father has long since called you blessed, and I have been honored to guard you."

"I did see you once," I said. "You helped me when my Honda died in traffic. You pulled the girls and me out of the street and into a convenience store parking lot. You looked weather-beaten and tired, and you wore denim overalls. Once we were safely in the lot, you were just gone, vanished—you and the truck. It was the most amazing thing. I knew instantly that it was you. Thank you," I said to my longtime guardian.

"It was always my pleasure, Tracy, I assure you. It will be my pleasure to stand with you as you train," he said.

"Train for what?" I couldn't help but ask.

"Train for what must be" was his reply as I raised an eyebrow to his mysterious answer. "Ah, the Holy Spirit comes," Ehren said as he bowed and took one knee.

I looked in the direction that my large friend bowed to see a warm glow appearing. Before my eyes, there she stood. She took form in front of me. My eyes could only associate her with feelings. She looked like comfort and kindness. She looked like a big hug. As she stood in front of me, she looked like a woman, with a woman's face and body.

"Yes, Tracy, my form is female. When I said, 'Let us create man in our own image and then create a woman from his rib,' where did you think I got the model?" She flashed a beautiful smile and turned toward my friend. "Arise, Ehren," the Holy Spirit spoke.

"My Lord," Ehren responded as he stood straight and tall.

"Travel with us," she continued.

Ehren nodded, and we were off.

CHAPTER 6

Looking Back

J ust then, the three of us stood at the end of my king-size bed. I saw my mother as she slept. Her cheeks were stained with tears. Next to her lay my daughter, Brittney. She looked worn and tired. I knew who they were, but I did not yet understand what was going on. I felt as though I was only to watch.

A knock was heard at the front door, and we were instantly there. As my sister opened the door, my best friend walked in. She looked beautiful, strong, yet sad. She looked tired but determined to be at this place, at this time. "How are they, Kim?" she asked.

"Still sleeping. I was just about to wake them. I could hear them crying most of the night. I wanted them to sleep as long as possible."

"What can I do?" Cynthia asked.

"You can put some coffee on and make a light breakfast, toast and eggs maybe."

Cynthia complied.

I turned to my two escorts. "Everyone is so sad. What's happened?" I asked. "Where am I?"

As soon as the words escaped my lips, we were there. I saw myself lying in a casket surrounded by beautiful white roses. I looked beautiful, if I do say so myself. My eyebrows looked great; they did a good job on me. I looked peaceful, almost pleasant—as pleasant as you can look in a box, I suppose. My hair looked good too; I was somehow pleased.

We were in a chapel; soft music was playing as people began to arrive. I saw so many people. I guess you really don't know how many lives you've touched until you see them at your own funeral. Every seat was taken (not to sound bigheaded), but I was really touched. Okay, it was a small chapel.

I saw my sisters enter from the back, followed by Brittney, my mother, Cynthia, the rest of my family, and Grady; he walked alone. The pastor opened the service with a prayer and then began to speak about my life. He spoke of all the good I had done in the world; of course, I didn't think I had been such a big deal, but I looked good on paper.

God had impressed upon me to be a giver later in my life, and he provided what was to be given. It was true that giving was its own reward. I felt exhilarated to be able to do for others, just to help those in need. I most often found myself smiling as I left someone God led me to help. I didn't need any payment, acknowledgment, or reward. I had written several books and had been a consultant and trainer.

I had a good life—okay, a good "later in life." My youth was nothing to write home about, but it was where God taught me a lot of lessons. In general, even though there were hard times, I'd had a good life. I'd spent the majority of it living below the poverty line, but God helped my mother and, later, me to be clever enough, wise enough, and determined enough to make our lives look like middle class.

In all the times I'd thought of what heaven and dying would be like, I'd never thought that I'd be attending my own funeral. The service was lovely, and there was both love and sorrow in the room. I would be truly missed. I knew that the Holy Spirit would bring comfort and healing to all those who mourned my death. As we began to leave, I saw my best friend hold my daughter in her arms, as if she were her own. I always knew it would be that way.

"I will leave you for now," the Holy Spirit said.

"Thank you for taking me there to see them once more."

"You will see them again, when the time comes." And then she was gone. Ehren walked with me a little while longer. We didn't speak verbally, but we said so much. He smiled; I smiled, and we laughed at the same time.

"I love it here, Ehren," I said.

"We all do," he responded. "I will see you again soon." And he was gone as well.

As I began to walk, I instantly found myself at a front door that was unfamiliar. I felt compelled to ring the bell. The door opened, and in front of me stood Princess Diana. She was beautiful, tall, and radiant. She looked at me and smiled. I returned one of my own.

"Please come in. I'm so happy you're here," she said.

I followed her into the huge mansion and was awestruck by what my eyes beheld. Inside the huge exterior was the interior of a quaint little cottage. In comparison to its outside, the inside looked like the home of a hobbit. My mouth hung open as I turned to her.

"Isn't it wonderful?" she asked. "So small and quaint. I have all my favorite things here."

"It looks like you," I said in return. "My first thought would have been something more fantastic, but it does seem like you now that I am in your presence."

She moved gracefully across the room to the lovely tea service she had on the table near the window. I noticed that she wore blue jeans and a pink T-shirt. "Won't you have some?" she asked.

"Yes," I said as I crossed the room to join her.

Here I was, sitting across the table from one of the most iconic figures in human history. I had taken some of my own fashion cues from pictures I had seen of her.

The princess and I sat and spoke for some time. We spoke about our experiences in this wonderful place and how it was nothing like we expected. I had been taught as a little girl that when I died and came to heaven, I'd be instantly different. The whole new "heavenly body" thing made me feel as though everything about me would be changed. I'd be turned into a praise-and-worship robot.

It wasn't that way at all. I was not a robot. I give praise to him naturally because I want to; we all do. I feel no pressure to; I just want to. Here, it's like taking a breath. Even when I am sitting at my piano or playing with my dog, I am in worship. The hairs on my head worship him. My skin worships him. While walking down the street, he communes with me.

Diana and I marveled at how magnificent, wise, thoughtful, and benevolent he was to all his people. How wonderful it was that he had set up such a place for all of us, a place of overwhelming praise and worship that lends itself to a child of the Father going home to the mansion he'd built for her just to chill. There was utter peace and happiness here. The princess and I wrapped up our time together knowing that we'd see more of each other.

"Thank you for having me," I said.

"Come by anytime," she returned.

Bum's the Word

I felt as if I had been in this place forever, but in God's reality, it had only been a moment. I had seen so many magnificent things and met so many people with whom I had always wanted to spend time. God is so good. He graciously gives the desires of your heart sometimes even before you know it's your desire. I have been taken to so many periods of time and been allowed to walk there as if I had always belonged. I've spent most of my time here in heaven with my mouth hanging open—everything is just so amazing. Bum and I sat in the clearing by the gates, and we talked about our lives. He told me how the Father had brought him and Grandmother Elizabeth together, and I spoke of James and me and how I met Grady. We talked about how each of us had come to know God.

"I wish I had been able to spend more time with you as your grandfather. I'm sorry we lived so far apart," he said to me.

"I know. Me too," I replied.

As we sat there, the sky began to light up with color. We sat motionless in the grass to wait for what was to come.

The continent of Africa was all around us. The lush jungles, the magnificent beasts—it was so beautiful. I stood to take in the full experience. I remembered that I had not the pleasure of seeing this while on earth. *This is turning out to be the least expensive trip I had ever taken*, I thought.

We stayed in this place for a while before I saw any human beings. Just then, I looked to my left to catch a glimpse of a young tribesman just as he threw a heavily decorated spear through my upper torso and into the gazelle grazing three feet from me. The tribesman followed his spear through my presence, as I stood transparent and motionless.

Bum looked at me and said, "That's so cool, isn't it?" The intrusion upon my person did not hurt me, but it would take time to get used to.

The young man removed his spear and prepared to take the animal back to his village. All at once, a heavy, roped net was thrown on top of him, and there was chaos. Four white men jumped on top of the net and began beating the young man until he could no longer fight. His hands and feet were tied much like the gazelle that lay dead next to him, and he was dragged bloody through the jungle.

Scenes of the capture of thousands of individuals flashed before my eyes. The brutality was overwhelming. The fear, the confusion, and the trauma of mothers, fathers, and children being separated were palpable. The whole scene was startling; it shook me to the core, yet I felt no need to cry out, no need to shed tears. I was in God's comfort and peace. I asked Bum why God did not intervene; he simply said, "The gift of free will." I could see how a gift so preciously given could be used for such destruction.

As we stood in the midst of all this, men, women, and children ran through my presence, and I could feel their desperation and fear—not my own, but theirs. Some were herded into cages, and others were shackled together and led to the beach and onto waiting ships. I turned to look at Bum, who, I could tell, had seen all this before. As I turned back, we were in the belly of a ship on the high seas. The stench of urine, feces, vomit, and sweat was almost too much to bear. I could hear their native language, crying, and screams.

I could hear the men being beaten and the women being raped. Throughout the long voyage, the dead and the newborns were thrown overboard into the cold, deep sea. In all this, I could see the angels.

They were there, comforting and keeping. They could not affect free will, but they were there. Bum and I stood as the men, women, and children were sold on the auction block. They were torn from their families and the people they had known all their lives. As they screamed and cried, they were beaten relentlessly. Even the children were beaten and bloody. They were splashed with water to remove the blood just before the bidding started, and they were dragged to the block. Some were sold individually; others, as a set.

Later, Bum stood outside as I entered the empty slave quarters. The space was small and cramped with only the earth underfoot. A space that looked as if it could hold only two or three housed eight; the conditions were deplorable. I noticed a small fire pit and a few pots. There were two makeshift cots and several mats on the dirt floor. I could smell the overwhelming odor of a hard day's work. As I stepped outside, the sky fast-forwarded more images of the atrocities inflicted upon these people, my people…God's people.

The images faded, and I was back on the grass near the gate, but now I was alone. I sat upright, and I was awestruck by what my eyes beheld. Coming toward me as if from a billowing cloud, there they were, dressed as they were when they were stolen from their home. As they walked, I heard the music from the grass turn tribal. It was praise and worship, but it was most definitely African.

All of them came toward me, but now they were proud, happy, and smiling. Some sat down next to me; others began to sing, and others, to dance. It was one of the most beautiful things I had ever seen. The ancestors spoke to me and called me by name; we talked for what seemed like hours. It felt like I had known them always.

As time passed, I saw that others had joined us, and we all began to dance and sing and praise the Father as he stood in the midst of us. It was heavenly…it was heaven. They sang in their native language and beat upon drums. I too began to dance and sing in the native tongue. We all danced around a roaring fire that appeared out of nowhere. The Father, Son, and Holy Spirit were all there singing and dancing.

The praise continued, and I saw James, Christopher, and Bum in the crowd with their hands raised. With every passing moment, the participants doubled and then tripled in size. It was all so glorious.

I walked away from the excitement to get a look at what was happening; the scope of it was enormous. I sat on a small hill and took it all in. *Amazing,* I thought. *Just amazing.*

CHAPTER 7

He Is Love

When the singing and dancing dissipated, I stood as the Father joined me on the hill; he took my hands and looked into my eyes. "You are my child, and you always have been," my Father said with such emotion.

I could do nothing but cry the tears I had held inside all my life for just this moment. Early on, in my walk with God, I'd hoped I'd be good enough to make it in. Midway through my life, I'd fallen from time to time but was still hopeful that his grace was indeed sufficient and that it would cover all my faults.

I must admit there were times that I prayed that he wouldn't take out some heavenly big pink eraser and rub my name out of the Book of Life. As I matured in my walk, I knew that I knew that I would be here with him. This experience was unlike anything I could have formed in my mind while on earth.

There is so much love here; he *is* love. Touching him, looking upon him, hearing his words to me—it is all so exquisite. If I could feel faint while in heaven, I would, but since I'm in heaven, I can't, so let's just move on.

"Father, thank you," I said, "for wanting me with you."

"Of course, I want you with me. I want you all with me. You *are* me."

"I *am* you?" I replied.

"Yes, Tracy, you are me, and I am you. We are all one."

The Father went on to say that just like we are all physically a part of both our mothers and our fathers, we are all a part of him. We all come from him. I understood exactly what he meant; I just wished I'd gotten it while I was on earth. It would have made things so much easier. The Father began to explain about all the gifts he supplied to his people.

"It still saddens me that the law of attraction has been so underutilized. You all got the law of gravity like it was two plus two. My people could have created and been and had so much more. I thought that the concept of 'you bring about what you think about' would be more easily understood and accepted than it is. All my children could have had unbelievable lives."

"I know," I said. "I wish I had learned the secret long before I did. It would have saved me so much time and trouble. Darn that Oprah! If she had found the secret sooner, she'd have put it on her show sooner, I'd have seen it sooner, and I'd have had a better life sooner, darn her. If I had known the power of my own thoughts, I would have had an Academy Award by my twenty-first birthday."

The Father got a chuckle from my last statement, and it made me smile. I was just about to ask God why he kept the law of attraction such a secret, but before I could ask, he looked at me and said simply, "The free will of my children."

"I never wanted anything to be a secret. A portion of the human race made those choices themselves, and yet another portion followed along without question and did not search for the truth," he continued.

I listened and realized that I couldn't blame Oprah or anyone else for my life's challenges, trials, and downright failures. I had always had the mind of Christ and was made in God's own image. It was my choice not to use those gifts to build the life I had dreamed of early on. I didn't study to show myself approved.

What we all had been taught about God and who he is and what he wanted, while we were on earth, was so full of misconceptions, misunderstandings, and just plain falsehoods. Generation after generation was led to believe so many outlandish things. We were taught that God, in his infinite wisdom, would actually give us so many wonderful free gifts, then test us throughout our entire lives, and then condemn us to a fiery, everlasting existence because we tripped and fell while utilizing his gift of free will. He had always given us a way out and a way home.

Throughout my lifetime, I was led to believe that this most loving Father would be more disappointed in me than I could ever be in my own child and that he would have me set on fire forever for messing up. I hated to spank my daughter in the effort to teach her right from wrong, let alone setting her ablaze for not getting it right in time. If through Jesus we came to him, I now understood that no matter where we were in our walk, he'd always give us the moments we needed to make things right before we drew our last earthly breath. It was our responsibility to pay attention and make the right choice. I realized in this place that if I had spent eternity separate from him, it would have been by *my own choice*, not his. The realities had become so clear in this place. God always was; we always were. We were and always will be a part of him. The conversation with God did me good; it was so amazing that I was actually having face-to-face dialogues with the Father, the one I'd spent so many years fearing.

It was not the healthy kind of fear that you have for your mother who let you know that if you even thought about embarrassing her in the grocery store, she would indeed break off your arm to beat you with it. The fear I was brought up to have for God was the truly scary kind of fear that had me ducking the lightning bolts that he must have been preparing to throw at the top of my head for the ridiculous, misguided things I did. I didn't like the feeling and was somewhat confused by it.

The whole "God is love" thing didn't quite jive with the whole "If you don't do what I say, I'm going to throw you into this hot, smoldering lake of fire."

"It has been just as amazing to all of us as it has been for you," Ehren said as he stood next to me. "Thinking that the Father would want you or anyone to burn for eternity is crazy. That's a long time, and how does the Father get any praise or glory out of that? Yes, you have to prove yourself worthy of this place, but the scare tactics you all go through are unbelievable."

As I looked at Ehren, he appeared to be getting a little riled.

"Sorry, that just gets my feathers up," he said.

"Will you travel with me?" Ehren then asked me.

"Sure," I said. "Where are we off to?"

"I need to accompany Coren below, and I thought it would be good for you to come along," he said as we began to walk.

Hell Itself

We met up with Coren on Angel's Row. *She is so beautiful,* I thought. Ehren looked toward me with the look of knowing what I had just thought.

"Are we ready?" she asked. I nodded, and we set off. We arrived at the bedside of a young woman. She lay in a hospital bed, and there were doctors and nurses all around her; machines were making loud beeping and buzzing noises. Just then, our location changed. The young woman, Annabelle, stood next to Coren, and I stood to the right of Ehren.

This place was unfamiliar to both Annabelle and me. Ehren looked down at me to say "Stay quiet and stay close." I nodded a silent "okay" in response and grabbed the hem of his loincloth much like a child grabs for its mother's hand. This place was shocking, and I could smell sulfur in the air. There were screams all around me, and I could see fire and smoke. I didn't feel any heat, but I could see flames in the distance. As we walked, I could see the terror in Annabelle's eyes. I realized exactly where we were. It was hell. Coren was taking her charge on a trip to where she was headed. Annabelle had turned from her religious upbringing long ago. Her stepfather's late-night visits and her prayers for his death going unanswered fixed all that in her young mind. We stood there motionless, me taking it all in.

"Observe," Coren said silently to Annabelle, who stood trembling beside her.

51

I looked around as Annabelle did, but I felt no fear, and I did not tremble. Ehren's hand on his sword let me know that while my salvation was secure, we were still *in* hell and on enemy turf. I stayed close as we walked on. I was amazed that even here, I could see the truth. I witnessed demons torturing the inhabitants of this place, and I could see them for their sin. I saw murderers experiencing the very thing they had inflicted on their victims, but much worse and much more violent.

The man being tortured before me had shot a man in the chest after robbing his store. The demon, Ratin, shot the man, and before his victim could even hit the ground, Ratin closed the distance between them as he pounced on his chest and began ripping at the man's bleeding wound with his claws to retrieve the same bullet he had been using since the man's arrival.

Ratin's victim screamed with pain as he was being torn, and then within an instant, the victim's chest was closed with fire, and it all repeated again. In this place, I witnessed the plight of rapists, child molesters, liars, cheaters, and nonbelievers. It was all so much to take in. I knew that this punishment would last a thousand years and at the end of all that, they would be thrown into a literal lake of fire, and still, they would never die.

As I viewed this like one of my movies, I noticed that it wasn't the same experience for Annabelle. Her salvation was not secured, and Coren knew this was the only way to open her charge's eyes. As Annabelle listened to Coren, she felt a hand grab onto her ankle.

"Help me," the voice cried out. Annabelle screamed and hung on to Coren. Just then, we were back in the hospital, with Annabelle lying in the bed, with the doctor saying, "Clear." The electricity surged through Annabelle's body; her heart began to beat, and she began to breathe. I knew that I would see this young lady again, in the place I now call home.

Back in heaven, I knew how blessed I had been all my life. It was sometimes hard to see it as I went through the day in and day out of life, but now I knew. Ehren and I talked for a while about what I'd seen, and it was clear to me that the human brain could not truly comprehend hell for what it really is. It would be no picnic for those calling themselves Satanists or atheists; they would know the truth soon after their deaths. Those who were willing to sell their souls, looking to share in Lucifer's wealth and power on earth could have no real idea of what is in store. The king of hell had no allegiance to them. No movie or TV show could truly depict what I saw in that place. There are no rewards, no virgins—just torture, pain, and suffering for a thousand years until they are judged and thrown into the fiery lake to burn forever. I dropped to my knees to pray for those not yet doomed. I prayed that someone could make it through the hard shell of sin they may be wrapped in before it was too late. Ehren joined me, and we wept for them.

CHAPTER 8

The News

Later I began to walk toward my next adventure when the sky began to light up with colors, and I took a seat in the clearing. The smell of roses wafted through the air. The white roses that encircled the clearing seemed to grow and release their scent just for me.

As the picture came into focus, I could see myself in the reptile house at the Fort Worth Zoo. I was with him; it was our first date. I looked good. I wore a white flared miniskirt and a navy-blue sailor top, complete with one of those flaps on the back. I even topped it off with a white sailor hat! Hey, it was the eighties—need I say more? I didn't know then the amount of hell I'd put this man through before it was all over, how much hell we'd put each other through. We shared our first kiss there among the snakes, frogs, and lizards. The pictures began to fly by at a fast and furious pace; I took in so many things. The pictures slowed down to the night our daughter was conceived—on the floor in the laundry room of his parents' house (I know, romantic). There, surrounded by my future father-in-law's undershirts, the Tide and Downy, my precious Pooh Bear was created.

At that moment there in the clearing, I could feel the emotions we both were going through. I saw images of this young man doing so many ordinary things, but all these ordinary things were tied to his emotions. I could feel how he felt when I told him about the baby— excited but freaked out and worried.

I didn't know all the things I needed to know about him; I didn't know the things he'd been through with his father, which would come out as he parented his own child. I didn't know that he truly needed as much attention, if not more attention than I needed. I would resent him for that. For making me the butt of his jokes and diminishing me. For not taking care of me, and for scarring me almost as deeply as my father had. As the pictures moved on, I could see myself as I broke the pregnancy news to my mom and sister. I was trembling; I was worried and ashamed and scared. My sister didn't help by calling me stupid as she stormed out of the room. I didn't know then, but she did not want me to have the life she had created for herself two years earlier. Telling them both was one of the hardest things I'd ever do.

I didn't know how to be anyone's mother; I was hardly a successful twenty-year-old! As I was taking this trip down memory lane, I could see Ehren visibly in the pictures. He was just outside the laundry room door, making sure that Brittney would arrive safely. He was with me as I broke the news to her father and to my family, and he was there on the day of her birth with Reardon, the one who would walk with her all her days.

My marriage was a hard one; it lasted eight years too long, but the necessary divorce would be a blessing to us both. We were young, and we hurt each other so much, our actions stemming from our paternal relationships. He had a very dysfunctional one; I had none at all. As I looked at these pictures, I was overcome with tears, with emotion that I had not felt here in this place. I felt bitterness and anger and desperation. I felt longing and sadness and a huge void. I could not understand these feelings as I fell to my knees. I was helpless to stop the tears. I cried and cried and cried. I could not understand what was happening. Why was I so overcome? How could I shed tears and feel so terrible in this place? As I felt the tears, I felt them arrive. They gathered around me as I could hardly breathe through the episode.

"Why?" I pushed out as I stood to face them.

"My child," the Father said, "what you are going through is what you needed to go through so many years ago, but you never released it. We have been with you, waiting for you to let it go so that you could live your life to the fullest, but you never did."

I felt so human and ordinary at that moment. I was actually on the verge of being angry that they would do this to me. They all looked at me, and I knew that they could feel my anger with them, but I could also feel beyond all the tears and the hurt and anger that, through this, they loved me.

The sky lit up again as the Father and the Son left my presence, leaving me alone with the pictures of my life and with the Holy Spirit. I knew we both had jobs to do. My job was to take a good, long look at the relationship with my father that I should have taken while on earth. Hers was to comfort and strengthen me when I wanted to look away or fall apart. The introduction into each of the previous "movies" was breathtaking. The colors and the light breezes were intoxicating. The opening to this one was longer. I felt the same comforting breeze I'd felt on my fingertips earlier, but this time, it ran all through me like I was being reinforced for what was to come.

The Second Floor

The longer I stood in the colors and in the breeze, the stronger and more fortified I felt. I turned to thank the Holy Spirit for what she was already doing in preparation of what was to come. She gave a comforting smile and a tilt of her head.

The colors dissipated, and I could see the two-story building in Detroit that housed my mother and her three daughters on the top floor. The second-floor apartment was now wrapped around me. I was back there. I remembered it so vividly even though I was just seven when we moved away.

The house stood silent; it was a little while before I saw my mother walking from the back of the house to the kitchen. I heard my sister's voices before I saw them run toward the front door, Kim with the jump rope in her hand as Debbie followed. I walked toward my mother as she stood at the kitchen sink. She was so young, so beautiful. She looked a little tired, but she did have three daughters, all under the age of eight. As I stood there admiring my mother, I heard weeping. Okay, it was full-on, little-kid crying. It was the kind of crying no one wants to hear in a movie theater or on an airplane. It was weeping and wailing. It was, well, me. I walked through the house to find my three-year-old self sitting on my little-girl bed with a face full of tears and snot. "Tracy," we both heard my mother call to me.

I watched as I scooted off the bed and walked toward my mother's voice. She knelt down to wipe my face with a clean kitchen towel. "Tracy, I know you want to go outside with your sisters, but they're not big enough to watch you, and I just can't go out right now. Can we go out tomorrow?" she said with a smile and a hug.

I nodded as she picked me up and gave me a hug just as there was a knock at the door. My mother held me as she went to the front door.

"Hey, girl," the big man said as his bigger-than-life form filled the doorway.

My mother seemed to know this person, but as I stood watching, I could not recall his name, and his face was not familiar to me. Being sent back here from heaven, I thought all would be revealed to me, that I'd be able to see everything. This man, there was something about him, but even in my present state, I could not recall what. I could do nothing but let the past play out.

My mother put me down as the man took a seat in one of the dining room chairs, and they began to chat. During the conversation, she said his name, but it was silenced as if covered by parental control on a television. The conversation continued as my mother disappeared into the kitchen. There were two arched openings with an expanse of wall in between that separated the kitchen from the dining room, which made conversation easy but eye contact impossible, unless standing directly in one of the arches. As my mother and her guest continued their conversation, I saw the man hold his arms out and motion for me to come to him, and I complied with a smile as most three-year-olds would.

As I watched, I realized that I knew this man. He had been in our home before, and he was considered a friend. My spirit felt compelled to move closer to get a better view of what was happening. My mother continued to laugh and talk to the man who sat in her dining room with her three-year-old daughter on his lap. They continued to talk as he slid his hand under my dress and his finger into my ruffled panties. Just then, I saw Ehren and the Holy Spirit. I saw Hendrik and Sedren as they stood for my mother and the man. Even at my tender age, I knew something was not right. I saw both the man close his eyes and the expression on my face. I was helpless to come to my own aid, and I understood what all the spiritual beings in the room must have felt. Just then, I heard my mother's voice come closer, and the man's finger was pulled clear of my body, and he put me on my feet just as my mother entered the room. I hurried to her, and she picked me up. I hugged her neck tighter than I ever had. I was scared, but I could not voice it. I just needed to be wrapped around my mother, the safest place on earth.

The man left moments later, and as I was being held in my mother's arms, the three remaining beings encircled us and began ministering to me. I watched this display through teary eyes. To watch these heavenly beings comforting and taking care of me in such a loving, kind way was overwhelming. Little did I know that Ehren was taking the memory of the violation from me until I was old enough to revisit this place again. I looked around the room, and I knew where I was, where my mother was, and where my sisters were. What I did not know was, Where was my father? Where was he when the man made himself comfortable in this home with his child? Again, the pictures came fast and furious, all of them minus Lee Palmer. I realized that the day the man visited our home was the day I began to resent my father and his absence from my life.

Throughout the years, my father's absence tore my insides to shreds. How does a man justify not wanting and being responsible for his own children? As the pictures flew by, I could see my effort to reach out to him so many times—and so many times, I saw the excuses and his lack of effort. I saw the pictures of his life; I saw this man being raised by his parents, a womanizing father and an overbearing mother. In this time of reflection, I began to see that my father was simply a product of his upbringing. He had been a horrible, cheating husband and a disappointing, absent father. I had never taken the time to look at what he had been faced with, which was surely instrumental in building the character of the man he had become. Marrying his third wife and creating his fifth daughter did nothing to make him a better man, at least not for daughters 1, 2, 3, and 4.

The Father was right; I had not dealt with it. I realized that I had been so mortally wounded by my father's abandonment that being in this place with the Holy Spirit was the only way I could truly let it go. On earth in the physical, I was a big open wound that never healed because I could not release it. The Holy Spirit held me as I cried—not just for myself, but for all the little girls who just want their daddies to come home. The Father and the Son joined us as I shed the tears and the pain I had carried far too long.

Pain, heartache, and tears were the last things I expected in this wonderful place. God shows himself to be more loving with each encounter. I had not allowed myself to release my father's sins against me prior to my death, but still, the lesson had to be learned. I would live for eternity, and God would not allow that unlearned lesson to follow me into what he had next for me.

CHAPTER 9

And So It Begins

Later, I heard Ehren call my name, and we were instantly away from that place and hiking on a mountain trail. The air was crisp and clean. In my life, I had never gotten so much exercise as I had in the short time since my death. I wondered if it was God's way of getting the sedentary to walk without complaint. Ehren and I walked for a time, inaudibly speaking to each other like old friends. As we walked along the trail, I began to hear noises. The sounds of metal meeting metal, laughter, and angel's wings seemed to be all around me. I slowed my pace and was preparing myself for the movie that was about to play. I settled myself comfortably, lying back on a small hill that jutted up from the hiking trail. I was surprised to see Ehren continuing on up the path; he was about half a mile away when he discovered that I was no longer by his side. Ehren took one step and closed the distance between us.

"Why have you stopped?" he asked as his shadow covered me and the gracious little hill I had relaxed upon.

"I'm waiting for the movie," I said, looking for the colors to appear.

My huge friend began to laugh—not a little "hehe" or a chuckle, but a big angel belly laugh. I shot to my feet and gave him a look that let him know that I was missing the humor of the situation.

"This is no movie. I have brought you here to begin your training." He pushed out as he tried to regain his composure. "Thank you, my friend," he said to me. "I haven't laughed that hard in a million years."

"My pleasure," I said, a little reluctantly.

The large angel tousled my hair, and we moved on down the path together. As we walked farther down the path, we came upon a clearing. There, in the midst were several angels and their charges. There were horses and swords and shields. The angels were teaching their charges how to connect with and ride the heavenly horses and how to wield the swords with power like expert swordsmen. I could feel Ehren's eyes burrowing into the side of my head as I watched the events.

"Well?" he said.

"Well, what?" came my reply.

In the blink of an eye, a majestic winged chestnut stallion stood before me. He bowed his head to me, and I bowed to him; it only seemed right. I knew this horse would stand with me in whatever was to come. Carlo was his name, and he was magnificent. He looked so strong and powerful but at the same time sweet and gentle. Carlo knelt down to allow me to mount him. I was amazed at how comfortable I felt in his saddle, behind his massive wings. Carlo started with a trot, and the more comfortable I felt, the faster he went. In a short time, we were in full gallop. I could not help but giggle uncontrollably; I felt so happy and free. Carlo took me to the far side of the clearing, and we rode a while in total silence although we were in constant communication.

My new friend spoke to me about his role in what was to come. He told me that he would run fast and stop on a dime when needed. We would fight on land as well as in the air. He would be an extra pair of eyes in my defense when the enemy's weapons attacked. Should I need to dismount, my stallion would remain close and keep my protection utmost on his mind. Throughout this conversation, I knew that my role would be explained to me as soon as we returned to the group. I was eager to learn because I knew what battle we were preparing for. It was just so surreal that I was here now, training for the last and greatest battle to be fought: Armageddon. When I had first been told of the battle, I had visions of how cool it would be to be fighting alongside the Lord and his angels. However, I never imagined that I could be injured. "Injured in heaven"—that statement didn't sound feasible, but the more I thought about it, the more it made sense.

This would be a battle after all, and there would be combat. All around me, there were swords, crossbows, shields, breastplates, and helmets. I could actually get hurt here, but I knew that my life could not be ended. If injured, I would need to be healed, but what better place for it? What we were all fighting for, whom we were fighting for would be well worth the sting of any sword. Ehren and I sat awhile to discuss what was to come and what would be involved in my training and how often I would train. This would be a battle we would all enter into willingly, and the Father wanted us to be prepared. Ehren told me of the history behind the upcoming battle and explained the need for it. It made more sense coming from my huge trainer than from any religious scholar who had ever made reference to it. We talked a little more before we resumed our lessons. Ehren, Carlo, and I trained for what seemed like days, but I was not a bit tired or drained. In my life, I would have been admitted to a nearby hospital for exhaustion, but here in this place, I was exhilarated. Throughout training, I'd felt more power, passion, and intensity than I ever had in my entire existence. As Ehren and I fought with the swords and shields, he taught me many ways to protect myself—that is, after he had pierced me between my ribs. I felt the heat from his blade as it cut through my presence. As Ehren withdrew the blade, a shaft of light escaped my being. It was remarkable. By the time we were finished, I was lit up like a Christmas tree.

Later, all the angels and their trainees gathered in a circle on the field as the Holy Spirit appeared in the center. All the wounded trainees lit up the field like the parade of lights at Disney World. The Holy Spirit extended her hands and healed us all in an instant. Just then, the Holy Spirit began to clap her hands. One by one, the angels joined in, and all together, they gave an overwhelming applause to their freshly healed warriors. As the ovation continued and became louder, I realized that so many others had joined us. The size of the gathering resembled the one I experienced in the stadium when I first arrived. What started as an ovation to tried and tested trainees turned into praise and worship of the Father. That's how it seemed to happen here. It's just spontaneous and comes out of nowhere. We didn't have to be gathered in a church setting or with any formality. Praise could begin while just walking down the street, alone, or with others. But wherever it happened, as the Bible says, "God inhabits the praise of his people." He was always there not just enjoying the praise but actually taking part. He sang and danced, lifted and clapped his hands as we all did. He inhabited the praise. I was just in awe of him.

Paris

After taking an early class with the disciples, I took a long walk with Mokie. As we walked, I realized that I could think of a place, and there we stood in its midst. Just then, I felt a warm springtime breeze as I approached and took a seat at a café on a street in Paris. Mokie lay comfortably at my feet.

As I sat there, a young man approached me with an array of delicacies I could never have hoped to feast upon. As I finished one, he'd bring me another. I thought as I consumed the tasty dishes, *Heaven is a sweet deal.* All the earthly trials and tribulations were so worth it, even though at that time, they left more to be desired. All the good things that I thought heaven would have don't compare to the reality of this place. I looked down at Mokie to find her sampling the best of French cuisine too. Once we'd finished stuffing ourselves, we took a walk. We saw everything I'd ever thought of seeing. The Eiffel Tower, the Champs-Élysées, and the Arc de Triomphe were even more spectacular than I thought they would be. I had to get up close and personal with each of them. I could feel the stone of the Arch under my hands and the coolness of the steel that comprised the Eiffel Tower. The activity of the Champs-Élysées filled my eyes and my mind.

We were actually in Paris with the sights, the sounds, and the people. I carried on full conversations in *French*. There was a different air here. I finally realized that Mokie and I were actually in Paris, France, on the continent of Europe on the planet earth. We weren't in some holy virtual reality. We were actually walking on the streets of Paris. I had to sit a minute and just take it all in. God was more magnificent than I'd ever thought.

After giving me so many exciting experiences, he gave even more than I thought was possible. I had died, gone to heaven, and now I was back on earth in the twenty-first century, spending a wonderful day in Paris. Doesn't that beat all? Then something miraculous happened; coming toward me with a smile and several shopping bags was my daughter, Brittney. At first, I thought she must have recently died, but I could not see Reardon anywhere, and I knew he would remain near even in death. I looked up to find Ehren looking down at me.

"She is dreaming of you," he said. "All is well, and have a good time."

Those words allowed me to spend the day with my girl. We did more shopping and sightseeing. We went to Versailles, the birthplace of etiquette. It was fabulous to stand in the very gardens where my career had been born. Being a professional etiquette consultant had brought me such happiness and introduced me to so many interesting people. Being the etiquette and protocol consultant to the was an honor beyond compare. Brittney and I took a seat on a beautiful blanket set up for a picnic in the very garden where Louis XVI held his first outdoor party to introduce his etiquette concepts. I leaned back to feel the sun on my face. I was in heaven, I was in Paris, and I was with her. We talked and expressed our love for each other, and I spoke of so many things I'd wished I'd said before my death. We spent the entire day in the city of lights, and we had a wonderful time. We found ourselves that evening at the world-famous Moulin Rouge. Even in a dream, how could we come to this exciting city without coming to this exciting place? Upon crossing the threshold, Brittney's dream put us right in the middle of the first big musical number from the movie *Moulin Rouge* starring Nicole Kidman.

There was music and champagne and excitement. There were rich colors of royal blue, red, purple, and gold. We laughed and ate and sang the night away. I had the best time, and I think she did too. With that, she was gone, being awakened by her alarm clock. I was allowed to see her waking with a smile, but she looked tired.

"Why does she look tired, Ehren? Didn't she just wake up?" I asked.

"Yes, she's just awakened, but she did just spend the day in Paris with you," he said in a matter-of-fact kind of way.

Ehren spoke to me without uttering a word. He explained that while we dreamed, we were actually experiencing the situations our dreams create. That's why so many of us wake up tired and worn-out. Most have a hard time remembering because the time we spend dreaming is spent in another time and the two cannot exist in the exact same space. It was that simple. Something that God had made so simple, we made into something so different. The lessons I was being taught in this place were ever so extraordinary. I couldn't imagine that anyone felt worthy of them. All this had been so unexpected. It really was a total 180 degrees from anything I'd ever imagined it could be.

God himself was different from what I expected. Yes, I thought he'd be great and bigger than life, but he was so much more loving and compassionate, like the best dad ever—you know, the dad who kissed your knee when you fell from your bike, the one who opened doors for his daughter and taught his young son to do the same. He was like the one who let you talk seriously when you wanted to talk about the cute boy in chemistry class, and he didn't make you feel the least bit embarrassed. God was like that, only a million times better. I stood there just outside the Paris landmark and praised him. As I continued, others joined in, and as others joined in, there he was in our midst. We praised him in the excitement of the city under the lights of the Moulin Rouge.

CHAPTER 10

Swimming with the Fishes

After the exhilarating praise session, Mokie and I found ourselves walking back to the château. I looked down at my friend, and she seemed to be wearing the most satisfying grin, like the cat that ate the canary, or should I say, the dog that ate the French éclair. We entered the house, and I headed straight for the piano. Playing the piano gave me great pleasure. The clear notes filled all the spaces in the château. My home seemed to come alive when I played. The drapes and potted plants swayed as my fingers glided over the keys. I was so proud and happy that music came from my hands. That God had given this to me was so miraculous, so loving, so giving.

As I played, even Mokie moved to the tones of the piano. I spent what would have normally seemed like hours playing music I'd heard as a child. The music of Beethoven, Elton John, and the Gap Band flowed from my mind and into my fingertips. The experience was both wonderful and fascinating. I left the piano to walk the rooms of my beautiful home. The library was stocked full of any book I could ever imagine wanting to read, and the furnishings were overstuffed and comfortable; I could smell the leather bindings of the books.

I walked down the hall to find a small flight of stairs that led to a heated pool. It looked inviting although I never really learned to swim. As I entered the pool area, a white terry robe and a bikini replaced the clothing I wore. I looked down and realized what I'd always hoped was true…there are no stretch marks in heaven! The costume change gave me the confidence to just jump in. Okay, I didn't just jump in; I did a one-and-a-half gainer off the diving board! As I hit the refreshing water, I immediately opened my eyes. I could not have imagined what I saw under the surface of the water.

Floating past me was a huge blue whale and a school of multi-colored fish. I swam to the top of the pool to find the room I'd just left; everything was in its place. The surface was placid and clear; I was astonished. I lowered my body once more, and I began to swim. I hadn't had a lot of experience with swimming in the past, but it came so easily. I was surprised that I was able to breathe under the warm water. A multitude of sea creatures swam either with me or past me as I explored this new environment. I swam longer than anyone should be allowed to. I made friends with a dolphin and an octopus. I rode on the back of the blue whale that had made his presence known when I first entered the pool.

The water was crystal clear and blue. I spent time circling a beautiful coral reef, its colors bright and spectacular. As I swam, it sang praises to God just as the grass did. It was joyous. I swam a little longer before I made my exit from this fabulous world. I dried myself, tied the terry robe, and headed for the door. Upon crossing the threshold between the swimming pool and the hallway, my clothing returned, and my hair was dry and in place.

I walked farther down the hallway toward the delicious smell of fresh popcorn—with butter, no less. As the smell became stronger, I noticed, on a counter outside of a set of burgundy doors, a large tub of warm, buttered popcorn and a refreshing soda. My mouth watered; it was odd. It was not that I was at all hungry. I just felt the need to grab the bucket and the soda and make my way inside. It was a movie theater; "What did you expect?"

The Dance

As I entered what I could only describe as an opulent old movie theater, I noticed that the temperature was just right, not like ordinary movie theaters that were so cold it was like seeing a movie on Mt. Everest after leaving your parka at base camp. The walls were covered in burgundy velvet, and the seats were a deep purple. I had no idea what to expect. Would this be a new release or an old favorite? Would this be a film by M. Night Shyamalan or Steven Spielberg? I couldn't imagine seeing something by Stephen King, but after all I've seen and heard here, anything's possible.

I made myself comfortable as the giant screen lit up with colors—yes, those colors. The picture became clear as the colors began to fade away. The camera angle was as if I were walking through a forest. Of course, as in all my other encounters, I was actually in the woods, but while it was cold, I needed no covering.

There was snow covering some areas of the ground, and I could hear the earth crunch beneath my feet. The forest began to clear, and I could see barbed wire fencing, dogs, and soldiers. There were several wood-framed buildings and some others made of brick with smoke billowing from the chimneys. I realized where I was…It was Auschwitz.

As I walked through the barbed wire fencing, I was led to one of the large brick buildings. Before entering, I turned to look behind me. There, about three yards away, stood the Holy Spirit. I questioned her with my thoughts.

"Is this what I think it is?" I asked.

I could not imagine why I needed to be here…for this.

"It is where you think it is, but there are things that went on behind those closed doors that only those who experienced it and those in heavenly places are aware of. I want you to enter so that you will further know the love, grace, and mercy of your Father."

Outside I could see soldiers milling around, smoking, and laughing as I slipped inside. I passed through the doors to stand in the midst of about four-dozen people—men, women, and children. I heard crying and screaming. I heard fear. As I heard the sounds, sounds that could be heard from outside the thick walls of the grim building, I noticed that all the people I stood in the midst of were quiet; some were naked, and others wore rags. No one uttered a sound, and then the oddest thing happened. As if in a highly choreographed dance number, they began to twist and turn their bodies and lay themselves atop one another. This went on for several minutes.

Although I could still hear the screams, no one uttered a word. Just then, I saw the gas begin to rise, and as it rose, I could see the shapes of angels gathered around the room. It was from the angels that the screams and cries came. Turning back to the people, I could see that the gas that was meant to painfully destroy them had not affected them at all; the Father had taken them sweetly and quietly during the dance.

The sound effects made by the angels were for the benefit of those waiting and wanting to hear the cries. After a time, the gas dissipated, and the soldiers came for the remains. As they spoke cruelly about the dead, I knew what had really happened. I knew what my Father had done. Just then, shaken by a hand in my popcorn bucket, I looked over to discover that the entire theater was full with those who were the stars in the movie I had just watched. They had watched the images on the screen as I had watched what had happened to James. There were no tears and no regrets; there was just peace. They had been brought into this place as I had, as we all had. The images on the screen and the crowd dissipated as the lights came up. There was silence in the massive theater. I sat there alone with my popcorn, my soda, and the memories of what I'd just seen.

"So much of the world's history has been written from an assumption because the writer of that history was not actually present to witness the event," the Holy Spirit said as she appeared next to me.

"Yes," I said, "I think I am beginning to understand now." I walked from the theater in peace, thinking about what the Holy Spirit had communicated to me. All the historic things I had seen since my arrival had been so misstated in earthly history books.

I was amazed at how wrong we were about so many things. In our human form, we could not really fathom God's true goodness or his true intent in so many things. He is gracious beyond our capacity to understand his graciousness. If, in our human state, we could see God's work behind the scenes of our lives, we would simply implode for the inability to comprehend what our eyes beheld. God is a magnificent god.

CHAPTER 11

The Girl in the Blue Dress

I walked through my wonderful home a little longer before I stepped outside. Merkin and Chezen blessed me as I sat on the steps. I was there only a few moments before she arrived. The little girl in the blue dress, my little girl, sat next to me as I looked out onto the neighborhood. She was so beautiful, so precious.

"It's all right," she said. "I have always been happy here."

"I know," I said. "I'm just so aware of what was missed."

"Nothing was missed. I have always been with you. I was there when Brittney was born. I shared in everything."

"When you held her in your arms, you held me too," she continued. "When you taught her to walk, talk, and read, you taught me too. I know how much you loved and wanted me. I know why you did what you did, and it's okay."

The little girl I had reluctantly aborted that day talked to me as if we had been together always. I walked with her as she headed to the park where the other children played. I sat on a bench to take in all the action. The park was huge, and there were children everywhere. There was laughter, giggling, and horseplay. Children played on the merry-go-round and the slide. There were children from all spans of time. There were Cro-Magnon children playing with children that died during WWII. Children from the Holocaust played with children born into slavery in the South. I could not help but smile at the display. As I sat on the bench, I turned to find JonBenét sitting next to me. She wore a fancy royal-blue party dress and a massive crown.

"Well," I said, "don't you look pretty?"

"Yes," she said, "and thank you. When I got here, Jesus took me to my house, and there were dolls and games and other toys. When I opened one door in my house, I found tons of beautiful dresses and crowns. It was all so perfect."

JonBenét smiled as she told me more about her adventures in her new home. She spoke about the swings and slides room and the room where she could watch her favorite cartoons. We talked a little more before she ran over to play with the other children. As she ran, pigtails and play clothes replaced her dress and crown.

"She is lovely, isn't she?" Ehren said as he more than filled the space next to me left empty by JonBenét.

"Yes, she is," I agreed. *It is all so amazing*, I thought.

"Yes, it is," Ehren agreed even though I had not spoken a word.

"This place, these people…you, for that matter—it's all too much to take in. I find myself wanting more and more while, at the same time, I want for nothing."

As I sat there next to my friend, I thought about how happy I was that I was not in some eternal mass choir singing and chanting the same tunes over and over, that my reward in heaven was this place and not some weird praise-and-worship commune.

I was so happy that I had one-on-one time with each member of the Trinity whenever and wherever I desired. They were not standoff-ish; they did not rule with an iron fist from some mountaintop. They were approachable and loving.

"I know," Ehren chimed in with a smile.

"Is there anything you don't hear me say or think?" I asked.

"No. Is there anything you don't want me to hear?" he replied as we shared the knowing glance of longtime friends. As Ehren and I walked back to the château, I heard him call my name, and I was instantly in the presence of my Lord.

"Travel with me," he said as he extended his hand.

I quickly grabbed it, and we were instantly there. The room was dimly lit; the only light source was a lone spotlight positioned toward a makeshift stage. There were rows of folding chairs filled with people I recognized. I was overjoyed to see their faces again. They could not see me, but I sure saw them. Just then, I saw my cousin Carla appear from behind the curtain. She looked as pretty as she ever had. She stepped to the lone microphone in the middle of the stage, and this is what she said: "Good evening. I'd like to welcome you all to the twenty-second annual family talent show. We are happy that you could join us. We want to dedicate this year's show to the memory of Tracy Palmer, whom we lost this year. We miss her terribly." I could hear her voice tremble as it did after she welcomed the guests and dedicated the show to Christopher some years prior.

I looked at Jesus to say "Thank you for bringing me here," and he responded with a smile.

"Ehren and I have been to every show. You guys are hilarious! Remember when you did Britney Spears? Oh, that just killed me." The Lord began to break out in laughter; I was surprised and delighted.

The show began with Courtney playing her saxophone; she was great. I guess she'd been practicing since the last time I'd heard her play.

All applauded as she bowed and left the stage. Act after act was increasingly more wonderful. I didn't know if the ragtag group of performers had gotten so much better or if I was just so happy to see them all again. I walked through the crowd and saw so many people that had meant the world to me. My daughter, Brittney, was twenty-six, married, and pregnant with her first child. She looked happy and content. I stood so close to her that I could smell her clean hair. I kissed her cheek, and she reached up and touched the place where I had kissed it as if she could feel it being placed there. She turned toward me as if to look me in the face. Somehow, she could feel me there. She took her free hand and placed it on her belly as my granddaughter, Sofia, moved inside her. She smiled, and so did I. I resumed my walk through the crowd and visited my mother and my sister, Kim. They looked beautiful, and their additions to the show were as wacky as ever. I felt a tug at my heart, which caused me to turn and scan the back of the room. There standing against the back wall was Grady Tart, the man who had made me his wife. He was here in this place, in this city where I had been raised. I felt the Lord say "Go to him." As I approached him, his expression changed as if he knew or felt something. As I stepped close to him, he looked in my direction even though I knew he could not see me.

He placed his hands, palm side down against the wall as if he was trying to press into it. He had a feeling, but he could not put his finger on it; it was unlike anything he had felt before. I stepped to face him as I had done so many times before. I took his scent into my transparent nostrils; it was so comforting and sweet. Just as I laid my head on his chest, the loveliest thing happened; he crossed his arms, and when he did, I felt him hold me in his arms as I had every day of our life together. As he held me, the words "I love you, Tracy, and I miss you so much" could be softly heard from his lips. I looked up at his face and said, "I love you too." As I did, his eyes closed, and a satisfied look crossed his face.

I knew that he felt me say the words. I stood in the embrace for several minutes feeling his heartbeat and hearing the sounds of him breathing. As I stood with this man, the Holy Spirit and Roman appeared on either side of him, the Holy Spirit to bring him comfort and Roman to stand with him as he did at the funeral, as he always had. I stepped away from Grady as the Lord let me know that I had given what he'd brought me here to give. I could see a lone tear fall from the eye of the strongest man I'd ever known. Roman looked at me and nodded to let me know that all would be well with the man that I had loved for so long.

Missing Parts

As Jesus, Ehren, and I returned from the show, we couldn't help but talk about the many acts my family had performed over the years. We laughed about all the times Jay either was off-key or dropped a word or two from the Christmas song even though he had sung it for twenty years and how we had done almost all the tunes from the most popular members of the Jackson family. I think my mother had been Michael, Janet, and Latoya all within five years.

I was amazed to hear that they had been purposeful audience members in a family tradition that had meant so much to me since the beginning. While talking and reminiscing, I noticed that we stood in front of a majestic-looking building created with pillars, stone, and marble. The doors were carved from exotic woods.

"What is this place? It's beautiful," I asked.

"It is the missing-parts warehouse," Ehren replied.

Jesus took a step, and the massive doors began to open. At first, it was pitch-black, but then way in the distance, I could see the light of one lit candle then another and another. Before long, thousands of candles flickered and lit up the cavernous room. I looked around to see something I could only handle seeing in heaven.

This missing-parts warehouse was not filled with car or lawn mower engines or bathtubs or computer components; what I was looking at were body parts—human body parts…limbs and organs, to be exact. There were arms and legs of all shapes, sizes, and colors. What I saw wasn't macabre but strangely beautiful. So many questions formed in my mind instantly. *Why were they here? What were they for? Who were they for, for that matter?* This was heaven, and I hadn't noticed anyone in a wheelchair or on crutches. I looked to Jesus to find him already answering the questions just as he had on the field when I first arrived.

"These belong to my people," he said to me without uttering a word. "These are the parts that have been lost to them by accident or injury. Whether it was from disease, wrath, or war, the missing part is here." While Jesus looked around the vast room at the arms, legs, eyes, hearts, and other human parts so lovingly, I couldn't help but smile. "These will all be waiting for the owner to arrive or have the faith to call the part to his or her body while on earth." Jesus went on to say that no one has yet fully called their missing part and had it manifest through their faith, but one day, he will call for it, and it will appear. The last statement Jesus made brought such a twinkle to his eye I couldn't help but be elated. I could just picture a leg growing from a stump in the middle of the night and the owner of it waking to find the miracle that his or her faith produced.

"I knew you would understand," Jesus said.

"What do you mean?" I responded.

Jesus explained that a miracle like that would come in the dead of night, in the stillness and aloneness of human rest. Every physical system in the human body would be working at full capacity to welcome the new part and work with it as if it had always been. There would be enough excitement and activity once the new part was discovered.

I began to ponder that thought. What would happen when someone who went to bed with an amputated leg and woke up with a new one that looked and reacted exactly as the one that was lost? Surely that would provoke news coverage and questions and even a religious pilgrimage or two. I looked up, and yet again, Jesus was already speaking the answer.

While faith will bring the blessing of the missing part, it will sadly bring with it man's doubts and fears. Some will question the validity of the blessing, all while looking at it with their own eyes and touching it with their own hands. Some will find their own faith as a result and draw closer to me while seeing those closest to them run from the power of God.

God's wisdom and miracles were vast in this place and on earth. I prayed for the day that someone's faith would relieve the warehouse of at least one of its holdings.

As Jesus, Ehren, and I exited the warehouse, I looked back to see the last candle be extinguished and the space become dark before the massive doors closed behind us. Jesus blessed us, and then he was gone.

CHAPTER 12

The Battle in Faux

Ehren and I walked through the beautiful surroundings of this place. We talked a little more about the warehouse and about Jesus.

"What I have seen here is so cool," I said. "God has such a vast imagination and such interesting ways to show us his brilliance."

"How are you feeling today?" my large friend asked.

"I am perfect, but you already know that, don't you?"

Ehren answered me with just a smile.

"What's going on?" I questioned.

Giddy as a schoolboy, he answered, "There is a battle in faux that begins in a little while, and I think you should participate."

"What are you talking about?" I said as my eager friend looked to be jumping out of his wings in anticipation of my answer.

"On occasion," he spoke, "the Father allows us to put on faux battles for the new arrivals to practice their skills and for praise and worship, and one is about to begin. Will you take part?"

"You think I should?" I asked him. "I've been here such a short time, and I've only had one training session." I don't know why, but I think I was trying to get out of it.

"You will be fine. As always, I have total faith in you," he said.

"Okay, my friend. If you say I'm ready, then I must be ready."

My huge friend bowed his head to me, and I returned one of my own.

"Ehren, could I have declined to participate?" I asked.

"Of course, you have the gift of free will, and you shall always have it. Everything is your choice. Do you want to change your mind?" he questioned.

"No, not a chance," I responded, and with that, we departed to the coliseum.

On the way, Ehren explained as much as he was allowed.

"This is just a training battle, but make no mistake, it is a battle," he spoke seriously.

There would be real armors, swords, and shields; there would be real conflict, and Carlo would be there. Ehren made me wait to find out who we would be fighting. As this was not truly the last battle, I could not imagine who would be our opponents.

I could not imagine raising a sword to anyone that I had met in this awesome place, and I also could not imagine a busload of demons coming in for the big game. I'd seen demons, and I'd be very surprised if they would just be allowed to cross the threshold of heaven. I would just have to wait and see, but of course, I knew whatever the plans were, I'd be astounded.

We arrived at the coliseum, and it was vastly different from the first time I'd been there. The seating seemed to go on forever. Up, up into heaven it went. There must have been a seat for everyone ever created. There was excitement in the air. I had not yet comprehended what was about to happen, but it all felt so incredible. As we walked farther into the stadium, Ehren no longer stood next to me but hovered above, as did all the other guardians above their former charges.

We walked steadily toward the center of the field, and just before we reached our destination, I noticed that Carlo walked to my right, as did the other stallions with their warriors. When Carlo appeared for battle, so did my armor, sword, and shield. I'd thought that when we were ready to fight, our armor would all be uniformed and perfect. Nothing could be further from the truth. When I looked down at my armor, it was beautiful, but nothing any military would give to its soldiers for battle. The breastplate was a form-fitting, lightweight metal. It had the detail of tiny roses, encrusted with diamonds—not crystals or cubic zirconia, but diamonds. There were strips of pewter-colored leather that made up the skirt, which covered the pewter-colored shorts underneath. I mean, a girl has got to have a good pair of shorts in combat. My shoes laced up my calf and came equipped with three-inch heels. I know, you'd think I'd be wearing combat boots into a battle. While the ensemble was exquisite, I wasn't quite sure it was the best choice for what was to come. I looked up to ask the question to Ehren, who, by the way, was color coordinated with the "red carpet" look I was sporting, as was Carlo's saddle, bridle, and face mask.

Ehren answered without speaking, "The armor you wear will protect you as if you were in metal from head to toe. The color and the pattern, right down to the tiniest rose and diamond, are all the desires of your heart. There is not one thing the Father does not know about you. Your armor will serve you well in this battle and any other."

That was all I needed to hear. As I mounted Carlo, I had a full view of all the warriors; they too were armored in the desires of their hearts. Most appeared to have a warrior or military theme; still, others wore evening gowns, and some wore pajamas. I even noticed a tuxedo and a pair of flip-flops. All the guardians hovered above the warriors on their steeds as they spanned the width of the enclosure. Across them stood the inhabitants from Angel's Row; it was unclear what was to happen. Coren, the redhead, stood in the center. She was beautiful and exuded peace and the love of God. There were Keegan and Trenlow, Arlon and Breehaa. They and the others stood proud and majestic.

Just looking at them all, I could feel their concentrated love for me, as if I were the only one in the coliseum. I was sure it felt the same for all who stood before them. As the opponent's horses appeared next to their riders, the crowd began to applaud. The excitement grew. I was ready, but I didn't know how I could raise my sword to the magnificent beings standing across the field from me. My questions were soon answered. The coliseum exploded in praise as the Trinity appeared in the center of the field. We all clapped and worshipped them as they worshipped with us. The crowd settled as the Father began to speak about the battle and how this exercise will strengthen us all. As the Father and Son took their seats, the Holy Spirit remained. She faced the angels across the field and lifted her hands. As her hands rose through the air, the once beautiful and loving angels were covered in the facade of horrible, grotesque demons. Their eyes were yellow and bulging; their skin, dry and gray like cracked old leather. A foul mist escaped their mouths as they snarled and hissed at us. The beautiful Coren was transformed into the vilest-looking creature of all. As I witnessed the costume change, fully aware that what stood before me was Coren and all the angels that, only moments before, had my best interest at heart, I could not help but feel the need to obliterate what stood before me as God's enemy.

We Galloped Hard and Fast

As the battle began, the Holy Spirit took her seat in the stands, and Carlo took to the air, his presence strong and powerful beneath me. It was exhilarating, exciting, stressful, and frantic all at the same time. Warriors and demons were in full battle. I saw swords and shields everywhere; I was amazed.

"You might want to pay attention," Ehren said from behind me.

Just then, I felt his huge hand on the back of my neck. He pulled me back almost prone with Carlo just in time for me to miss the blade of the demon that was Coren. Carlo dived so that I could recover and get my head in the game. Both Carlo and Ehren accepted my unspoken apology, and I turned Carlo toward the opponent that obviously had chosen to take me on. Ehren returned to hover above. I would try not to need his assistance again. We galloped hard and fast as I lifted my sword and headed toward my nemesis. All the love I felt earlier was gone; now all I wanted was to defeat my enemy. The sound of metal meeting metal and the heat of battle pushed me on in my desire.

I felt the first sting of the metal slice my left forearm, and it released a shaft of light. I did not feel the excruciating pain as I would feel it on earth, but I could feel a sting, massive weakness, and a dull throbbing. I knew I could no longer hold the reins but had total faith in Carlo to lead us where we needed to go. My thoughts were his, and I needed only to think of the action, and we were off. I raised my sword and sliced through Coren's outer facade from throat to hip.

As she felt the sting, Carlo whipped around in time not only for me to slice through Coren's spine but for me to slit the throats of two other demons as they headed toward me. All three fell from their steeds and landed on the ground below. I looked down in time to see Coren and the other two leaving the demon facades on the battlefield where they lay. Coren looked up at me and smiled as she headed to take her seat in the stands. I could feel her saying "Good job." I was spurred on by her acknowledgment.

Carlo and I landed to join the ground battle, with Ehren still hovering above. As I rode through the battle, I raised my shield to prevent a demon's sword from meeting me. As the sword connected with my shield, the power it wielded knocked me from Carlo's back, and I was on the field. Everything on the field was chaotic and fast-paced. I turned to look for Carlo, and he was racing to my side. As he neared me, I reached for the saddle horn and was again mounted on him as if we'd never been separated. I felt a sting and weakness coming from my right side. I'd been hit. The shaft of light appeared from the wound as I cut through the demon before he could make his escape. Carlo took to the sky, followed by Rico. Rico's facade was huge; I didn't know how I would be able to take him. I felt so minis-cule in comparison. Up until this moment, I'd felt powerful and like I could do this, but now I felt only...small.

"What will you do?" I felt Ehren say.

"I don't know," I said. "He's enormous."

"What did you use to do when things were just too big for you to handle on your own?" Ehren whispered.

I could tell my friend was trying to get me on the right track. It took mere seconds to realize what I needed to do to even begin to defeat this enemy. I steadied Carlo, I bowed my head and closed my eyes, and...I prayed.

"Father, I don't know how to defeat this demon on my own. He's just too big. Please strengthen me as I face this obstacle to glorify you."

"Tracy," the Trinity returned in unison, "you are never alone. Ask and it shall be given. Raise your sword and ride true."

I opened my eyes and lifted my sword. Carlo took off in Rico's direction; he ran faster and harder than ever before. I met Rico's sword with so much power that sparks flew. The sword battle was quick, fierce, and intense. I became angrier with every blow. I had to defeat this foe that would come against the Father, against love and goodness and peace. Everything I had ever felt about evil and those who serve it was mounting inside. I could tell that in his facade, Rico wanted me too. He wanted to tear me to bits. I took a deep breath, fortified myself, and realized that even though this was just a training battle, it was him or me. Okay, his head was five times bigger than mine, and his arms and legs were the size of tree trunks. But no matter what, he was going down. I set my sword to Rico's massive chest. The speed with which it flew was astounding. I took out all my earthly frustrations on the leathery skin of his chest.

Carlo rode in circles around him as he aimlessly tried to make contact. Rico was a tough opponent, but he was no match for the will of God. I made one last strike to the base of his skull, and he slid from his mount to the field below. I watched as Rico fell and noticed that I was the only one left. Carlo, Ehren, and I stood in the open air alone. The other warriors had handled their demons and were now encircling the field below. The demon facades lay in their midst. Carlo returned to the field, and I joined the others and completed the circle. The stadium was on its feet. There were sounds of praise and cheering for the glory of God. Joining us on the field were the angels from the row that put up a tough fight, then Ehren and the other guardians, and finally, the Trinity.

The fallen facades were burned in holy fire, and the warriors were healed by the Holy Spirit as praise of the Father broke out. I was honored to be a part of this special time. The spectators from the stands began to fill the field as we all danced and sang praises to the Father of all. I did not know what to expect from this battle, but standing in the midst of all this, I could see the benefit of it. We all knew that through everything, we would stand and fight to defeat anyone who came against this place.

CHAPTER 13

Single Piece of Amethyst

After the battle and the praise session, I found myself walking again on the streets of gold. Man, I do a lot of walking.

I walked for a bit until I found myself in front of a round stone structure. Outside were massive columns wrapped in gorgeous climbing vines, dotted with roses that sparkled. As I approached, I could hear chanting, and I felt invited to enter. Stepping into the massive structure, I noticed a large round table made of the most magnificent single piece of amethyst. Around the table sat the twenty-four elders I remember the Bible referring to. The group all looked wise, aged, and oh so regal. The crowns with all the diamonds, rubies, and topaz didn't hurt either.

I allowed my eyes to drift above the table and its occupants to find a bright, warm light hovering over it. I looked into the light and saw God. My eyes were filled with the glory and the spectacle of it. As the elders continued to chant, the sound enveloped me; my whole being went limp. I felt my self being lifted from the ground and pulled toward the light and warmth of God. As I came closer to him, he began to swirl around me, and me, around him. We passed in and out of the others' being until we became one. In the space we shared together, I saw so much. I saw the creation of the planets and the stars, the creation and destruction of the dinosaurs, and I saw the laws of the universe created. I breathed in all I was experiencing. I felt the Father as he created all those incredible things. I felt his love for all he had created. All he has manifested has brought him joy. Those things that would irritate or try a human being only brought the Father joy.

Being a part of him, I knew instantly why. The Father took joy from everything in existence. As God released me from his being, I floated down gently and landed on top of the amethyst table that the elders still stood fast around. The experience left me exuberant. I don't know how I got off the table and back onto the street, but it was far from important. I smiled all the way back to the château as the grass sang and the trees swayed. I was lost in my thoughts as I walked through this wonderful city, this wonderful place. I began to hear leaves crushing under my feet, and I could see trees all around; the light that shone in this place could be seen through all the branches. I was in a forest—*a forest!* The closest I'd ever been to a forest on earth was walking through the tree-lined entrance to the mall. What I beheld was overwhelming. I was out of my element, but I was so comfortable. A sudden breeze blew through the area and lifted the gold, brown, and red leaves all around me.

As the leaves floated and danced in the air, they sang a song that was familiar but…not. It was beautiful and heavenly. I began to dance as music began to blend with the singing. I heard the sounds of nature and of water flowing. I saw birds and butterflies, and I couldn't release the smile from my face. I happily moved farther into the forest as flowers bloomed all around me with every step I took. The fragrance was enthralling. Every inch of my being was drawn into the experience; I felt full of joy and peace and happiness.

While walking deeper into the forest, I came upon a lovely sparkling river. It looked so inviting, inviting enough for me to touch it with the tip of my big toe. As the sparkling water touched my skin, I could do nothing but dive in. The water was cool and refreshing, not that I needed to be refreshed, but the feeling was there, and it was splendid. As I swam, I could see those who lived in this beautiful place. The mansions that God had built for them were here under this beautiful, refreshing water.

How magnificent and creative that this was an option when it came to having your mansion built. Continuing to swim, I figured that these homes were built for those who thought highly of the old TV show *Aquaman* and figured, "Why not?" I moved through the water with ease; it felt so natural. It felt natural to breathe in this beautiful water, and I could see clearly for miles and miles.

Liam

I met Liam as I swam. He looked to be about ten years old, and he asked if we could swim together; I happily agreed. While we swam, we talked. He shared with me some of his fantastic experiences since his arrival. When Liam arrived, he was met by his Uncle Michael, who was a famous ringmaster in the circus. Liam looked up at his uncle, who was fully decked out in his ringmaster's uniform; he couldn't help but smile. When the walls and doors of the long corridor fell away, Liam and his uncle stood at the entrance to the big top he had seen only once in his lifetime.

He was giddy, and he could not wait to see what was inside. The curtain opened to reveal a full-on circus complete with clowns, elephants, dancing bears, and lions. There were horses and trick riders, trapeze artists, and a man who spit fire from his mouth. As Liam told me of his circus welcome, I felt like I was there; I could almost smell the peanuts and cotton candy. After the story, Liam kissed me on my cheek and said we'd see each other again, and with that, he swam to the surface, climbed up on the shore, and was gone. I swam for a while after Liam left. I thought, Wow, *God is so sweet, compassionate, and thoughtful.* He knew that Liam loved the circus and that he'd only seen it once when he was four years old. How loving he is to have provided that for him upon his arrival.

"He is the most magnificent being," I said to Ehren as I felt him arrive.

"Yes, he is," he agreed.

As Ehren and I traveled through the water, we stopped and talked with Tally, and she welcomed us into her home. Tally Bishop arrived in 1936 when she was thirty-four years old.

She was tall and slender, with piercing green eyes. Her beautiful auburn hair flowed with the movement of the water. She welcomed us into her parlor, and as we sat, she explained that when she was a little girl, she loved the water and everything about it. Tally had been dreaming and thinking of this place for as long as she could remember. At every opportunity, she was in the water swimming, snorkeling, and scuba diving. She just wanted to be wrapped in water. For her, it was the most exquisite feeling. She began to tell us the story of her arrival.

When she arrived, she knew that the mansion that God built for her would be near the water, as it was her desire, but she never imagined...this. "When I got here," Tally spoke, "I was led to the forest you walked through, to the banks of this beautiful river. I looked all around, but I could not see my home. I knew it was here, but I couldn't see it. Then I turned to walk away, and there he was. God himself stood in front of me. He drew me to him, held me in his arms, and welcomed me. I was overwhelmed by the feelings of love and of happiness and of home. Just then, he propelled us both into the water. It was beautiful, and it sparkled all around us. I was still in his arms when I realized that I was breathing. It was the single most amazing experience. I knew I was home." As Tally spoke, she glided through the water, her arms splitting the liquid like angel's wings through the air. She was mesmerizing.

Tally continued to speak. "When the Father released me, I could see what lay ahead of me. It was the most stunning thing I'd ever seen. My home was made from a single piece of aquamarine, just a shade darker than the water surrounding it. It glistened and twinkled as if it were welcoming me. The Father opened the front door for me, and I entered. It was exactly what I wanted even though I could never really form it in my mind. The rooms were exquisite and just like...me."

"I know," I said. "That's how it's been for me too. It's all so surprising, but it's exactly what I wanted."

We all breathed a collective sigh at the brilliance of God's precision. After the lengthy visit, Ehren and I swam to the surface and walked onto the shore. As I thought of the things Tally had said, I was reminded of the conversation I had with the Father, how I was him and he was me, how we all are one. I learn something new with every experience here. I am consistently dazzled. I arrived at the château with the feeling of wonder and amazement. I had laughed and smiled so much since my arrival. In heaven, I had seen that anything and everything was possible. As each moment passed in this place, I was more astonished. I could simply think of something I wanted to see, and there it would appear. On earth, my thoughts were so stunted and so small, but here I could bring about what I thought about instantly.

CHAPTER 14

The People Who Stood before Me

After a while, I found myself and Mokie in a clearing on a beautiful, soft blue blanket. I saw before me many people—men and women, all different races and from all different spans of time. Somehow I could tell that the people who stood before me were once married to those they stood close to. Here, they were no longer married, but they still seemed to feel a connection, much like my connection to Ehren. He was no longer my guardian, needing to protect me; he was my friend, my buddy. I just wanted to spend time with him, and he felt the same way about me. These people were here for a reason, and I knew that I would soon find out exactly why. From underneath the blanket and all around me, I heard the grass as it sang softly. My attention was turned to the sky as it began to present its beautiful colors and the movie began to play. I saw, once again, the first two humans. Months after they were sent from their garden home, Adam and his wife were more in tune with each other.

Working together to provide shelter for themselves and talking long into the night strengthened their relationship and their resolve for what lay ahead. As I looked into their faces, I could see and feel how much they had grown to love and rely on each other. Day after day, the relationship grew; they worked the land together and enjoyed its small rewards.

As time passed, they learned more and more about the earth God created. Adam studied the land and remembered what the

Father said as he sent them from the garden: "The pain your wife feels in childbirth, you will feel in coaxing food from the ground." And he did feel the pain. Each day, he returned home with his body tired and beaten by the sun and by the soil. Eve would clean her husband's body as he stood gratefully in front of her. She poured the cool water over his naked body to remove the day's grit and grime. She laid his clothing outside for the sun and the breeze to dry and air out, and then she returned to her husband.

Adam lay on the bed of leaves and animal skins as his wife lovingly rubbed his sore muscles into submission; he liked this part of the day most of all. As the two made love that evening, I noticed Mihkile and Dailich covering the two under their massive wings; it was the most spiritual thing I had ever seen. It was not vile or pornographic; it was beautiful. Eve looked into her husband's eyes, and he, into hers; they expressed so much without saying a word.

As time passed, Cain was conceived and born. Adam and Eve, with the Father's help, learned quickly how to care for and protect the infant. Eve lovingly fed her son from her breasts as he grew strong and did the same for his brother, Abel. I could see the relationships grow in this first family: father to son, mother to son, brother to brother, and husband to wife. Through the years, Eve gave birth to more children, and the family was happy. It was fascinating to watch these movies play out, to watch them without the veil of human opinion, to only see what God truly intended.

The family sat together with God in their midst, and they talked about anything and everything. They asked questions of the Father, and he responded openly. The fact that we, throughout history, had lost that open, auditable speech with the Father was devastating. By leaning to our own misguided understanding, we stopped listening to what God had to say, and over a period of time, we stopped being able to hear his audible voice.

As in my other movies, the pictures began to move in fast motion, stopping just before the death of Abel. As Cain worked the land, he could see his brother constantly under his mother's wing. Abel would help his mother with the household chores, and he would comb her long hair. Cain could see the strong connection between his mother and Abel. One particularly hot afternoon, as Cain watched his younger brother, he began to feel something he had never felt before. It was odd, and he tried to shake it. As he began to set his mind back to work, he heard a voice.

"Wouldn't you like to be in his place, in the shade of the house and in the sparkle of your mother's eye?" The voice continued to speak, "Why should you be out here in the hot sun toiling while he combs your mother's hair?"

Day after day, Cain heard this voice, and soon the unfamiliar feelings turned into hatred and rage. Cain could not shake the feeling that as hard as he worked in the fields, nothing he did was ever good enough.

The feelings built up until the very moment Cain heard the voice say, "You could just get rid of him. It wouldn't take much effort at all. You have worked these fields long enough for your body to become strong and powerful while he is weak and powerless."

Cain took those words to heart and acted on them as soon as his brother was within arm's reach. Cain beat his brother repeatedly with all his power until he lay dead before him. It all happened so quickly, and Cain could not stop once it had begun. He didn't even remember picking up the jawbone. When it was all over, he saw what he had done, and for a few moments, he was in disbelief. Here on this earth he had plowed for years lay his brother, dead by his own hands. He was shaken back to reality by movement in the crops; he turned just in time to see the serpent slithering along the ground.

His voice caught in his throat as he yelled to the heavens, "What have I done?"

As I watched it all happen, I could feel the emotions of all the players. The choices that were made could not be taken back, only learned from. The admonishment from his parents sent Cain away from all he had known and sent him into the wilderness. The relationships between father and son, between mother and son had been broken.

While I Knew They Still Loved Each Other Terribly

Through the pain and misery at the loss of their son, the relationship between husband and wife became stressed. Instead of pulling together through the tragedy, they pulled apart. I now understood where it all came from. It had been none other than the serpent. One planted thought was all it took. The misunderstanding promoted by the serpent was the beginning of all misunderstandings. It seems that little grains of deceit, twisted truths, and selfishness are all it takes for the human race to turn against those they love and care about; the closer the relationship, the more hurtful the offense.

I watched Adam and his wife a while longer, their relationship strained. While I knew they still loved each other terribly, I could see that it was difficult for them to relate to each other. Pictures of their lives together began to fly by, and even though the pace of the pictures was a blur, I took in all the information. They both tried so hard, but on so many occasions, they both fell short. The pictures began to slow down as the Father visited the two one afternoon; they all sat out in Eve's small garden.

"What troubles you, my children?" the Father questioned.

"We are having such a difficult time with each other, and we don't understand why." Eve was almost in tears as she spoke. She held Adam's hand, and he gave it a gentle squeeze.

"The work gets done in the same fashion, but in the evenings where we used to talk, we barely say a word. It's hard. Sometimes, it's as if we were strangers."

Adam's words saddened the Father. God looked at his creations and felt what they were going through.

"My children," he said, "I feel your pain and anguish. What you are going through is an aftereffect of the original sin committed in the garden that day. Eve, do you remember when I said you will try to please your husband but it will seem impossible?"

Eve nodded the unspoken yes.

The Father continued to speak, "While there are consequences for your actions, there is always room for you to learn and to grow in wisdom in response to them."

Both Adam and Eve looked at the Creator with questions.

"What do you mean, Father?" Adam asked.

"Remember, Adam, when you first began to work the land, do you remember how hard the earth was?"

"Yes, I remember," Adam said.

"And when you found the earth hard and uncompromising, what did you do? You must have known that you couldn't simply leave it as is. You couldn't simply be exasperated by it, you had to…"

"Work at it," Adam finished the Father's sentence.

The Creator went on to explain that he created woman to be of help to man, not to be a burden or to be argumentative or for her to be alone. God created woman from man. God intended men and women to travel their lives together and to work well together. The fall in the garden changed things and, from that time on, made things hard. However, because the Father loves his children, his original plan for the relationship remains the same.

"My children, I have given you free will. The decisions that you make are your own, and they are my free gift to you. You may use your free will to dwell in the muck and mire of what this relationship has become, or you can use it to turn it around for your good. The decision is yours to make. You can work on this relationship, or you can simply let it be what it will be if you give it no attention at all. While making your decision, remember this: I am your father, and I will always love you. Nothing you can do will ever change my feelings for you. The consequences for your actions may not be desirable or what you planned, but the same free will that got you into a particular action can also resolve it. It is all up to you."

"Also," the Father continued, "I want you to know that I will always be with you. You may not see me with your eyes, but I am there. You may not want me there, but still I will remain. Circumstances of your own doing may lead you to want to sever our relationship, but I will always be your father, I will always love you, and I will *always* remain." As the Father made his last statement, he touched their faces and then faded from their sight, leaving the two alone to utilize the gift.

"Adam," Eve spoke, "why would we want to be separated from him?"

"I don't know," Adam said, puzzled. "I can't see that ever happening. He has been so good to us."

The two returned to their small home to work on the relationship they both loved. The disappearance of the Father brought with it the reappearance of the colors in the sky and the end of the movie. I was back in the midst of the couples. I noticed that they spoke and laughed together for a little while. Each pair then embraced and parted ways, some walking away, while others simply vanished.

I stood there a few minutes and thought about what I'd just seen and heard. I thought about relationships I'd had that were just given up on or allowed to fall away. I realized in this place that all I ever had to do on earth was to think about what I wanted from each relationship and then put in the work to bring it about. The more positively I thought about the situation, the more positive the outcome. God had set it up that way from the beginning. God had always made a way.

I walked on toward the next desire of my heart, not knowing precisely what it would look like, but I was fully aware that whatever it was, it would be fantastic and exactly what I wanted.

CHAPTER 15

Party Time

As I walked enjoying the sights and sounds of heaven, I stopped in front of the open-air stadium. The memories I had of this magnificent place made me smile, again. Beginning to walk inside, I could feel the past praise and worship. I could feel the excitement of the battle in faux, and I could still feel myself in Jesus's arms as he scooped me up when I first arrived. While still walking, I closed my eyes and lifted my hands in anticipation of the upcoming worship, and the funniest thing happened; I bumped into a yellow balloon, a yellow balloon that was held by a silver string that sparkled. I felt a bit silly bumping into the only balloon in the cavernous passageway.

"Excuse me," I instinctively said.

The balloon bowed to me much like Maxine, the butterfly, did for the Father on the mountaintop, and then it began to float away, and I began to follow. I walked about three feet, and the one balloon was joined by ten others, all of different pastel colors. Those balloons were soon joined by several more and still others as I continued to walk. Before long, I couldn't help but bump into the balloons that were now surrounding me. With every contact, I was tickled and couldn't help but giggle, and I noticed that the balloons were giggling with me.

Although I was bombarded by the balloons, I did not deviate from the path. My feet seemed to know exactly where I was going

although I could only see balloons ahead. While the giggling continued, I began to hear music in the distance, familiar music. I realized
that it wasn't the grass singing… This was a band, not just any band;
this was Kool & the Gang!

As I continued to walk, the music became louder as the balloons began to thin out, and the giggling dissipated. I found myself
at the back of the stadium as I had stood before, but what my eyes
beheld now was a bit different from what I had seen before. What I
was looking at now was…a *party*. This had to be the biggest house
party in the universe, but instead of CDs or records spinning, Kool
& the Gang were playing "Celebration" live on stage.

The atmosphere was electric, and I couldn't help but join in. As
I danced and sang, I noticed the balloons that welcomed me into the
stadium were now floating above the massive group with their spar-
kly strings dancing in the breeze. Hundreds of thousands of people
were there, and I knew everyone. It was, again, as if we had all grown
up together, and as we sang and danced, I realized that we had. We
had always known one another because we had all originally come
from the same place at the same time. When God said "Let there be
light," we were already in this place; we were already with him, a part
of him. As I danced, knowledge flowed into me just as it had before.
God did not create souls just before we were conceived by our earthly
parents; we have always been souls that resided in this place until it
was time for us to learn the lessons we could only learn on earth,
lessons we could only learn by being born. *Cool*, I thought. *So cool!*

"I agree!" Ehren said, yelling over the trumpets as he danced
next to me.

We both smiled while continuing to enjoy the music. When
Kool & the Gang finished up to thunderous applause, Earth, Wind
& Fire took the stage and began with their hit "September" and con-
tinued with their most popular dance hits.

I was having so much fun; I danced and laughed and talked
with everyone. Next up on the stage was Sister Sledge singing "We
Are Family." The happy memories of being young and listening to
these songs flooded my thoughts in this place. As the lyrics of the

song rang in my ears, the stadium exploded in applause and agreement that we are all indeed *family*.

I looked across the stadium to see Jesus holding a man in his arms as he had me, on my earlier visit to the stadium. I knew instantly that the man was wondering about the artists he'd just seen perform on heaven's stage. Jesus explained how they were living out a desire of their heart or they were in bed having a wonderful dream of reuniting onstage with their bandmates. Lying in the arms of Jesus makes everything seem perfectly…reasonable. I spent what seemed like hours at the party. I spoke with so many people, and it was like we had always been together. We laughed, danced, and worshipped. I noticed something that I had not recognized when I first arrived; we were all here together at the party, but we were not all seeing the same performers or hearing the same music. We were all hearing the music and seeing the performers that were the desires of our hearts. Again, I couldn't help but think that God was absolutely wondrous.

You Are Amazing

Walking toward the château after the party, I felt Ehren arrive and begin to walk beside me.

"Did you have a good time?" he asked.

"You know I did," I responded. "Good times seem to be around every corner in this place."

Ehren and I walked on a bit before he broke the silence with "Will you join me on the row?"

Without hesitation, I asked, "Angel's Row? Of course, I will."

In a blink of an eye, we were there; seeing them in flight above me was so incredible. I felt honored to be in the presence of the miraculous beings. They were all so full of God's grace, and God's love showed on all their faces.

"Do you want to go up?" Ehren asked.

"Ah, yeah" was my quick reply.

Ehren knelt and allowed me to climb on his back and wrap my arms gently around his neck. His huge wings kept me from wrapping my legs around his waist, but it felt perfectly normal for me to simply be suspended from his neck. I adjusted myself so that I could comfortably see over his right shoulder.

"Ready?" he asked.

"Ready!" was my response through a toothy grin.

With that, Ehren bounded into the sky, and I could not stop myself from giggling like a schoolgirl. I felt the wind rush over me, and it smelled of cotton candy and then of hot chocolate. I felt like a bird soaring through the sky of heaven. We went everywhere. We did a swan dive and flew around planets and galaxies I never knew existed. We flew around the sun, and we landed on the moon. I stood near the boot prints of Neil Armstrong and Buzz Aldrin; I stepped into the famous prints much like a tourist would at Grauman's Chinese Theater.

"Hop on," Ehren said as he knelt down for me.

"Next stop, earth."

I didn't know where on earth we would end up, but I didn't care. This adventure was amazing. Ehren flew us to places I'd never been during my lifetime: the Amazon Rain Forest, Machu Picchu, the Great Pyramid of Giza, and Oxnard, California. I think he threw that last one in for laughs, and yes, I laughed.

I was so happy in the presence of my friend. No matter what we did together, it was made all the better because of his participation. I was so grateful that he has always been my guardian and that he knew me so well. Being with Ehren comforts me because I have the living proof that Rearden is watching over my daughter and keeping her safe. God is so awesome to have created these beings and to have given them such an important job.

I love my friend so much, I thought.

"I love you too."

CHAPTER 16

I Will Never Fall Asleep

I had been in heaven for some time. I'd seen so many fabulous things and met many extraordinary people I'd never dreamed of meeting. Mokie and I reentered the château as we had so many times before, climbed the stairs, and entered my luxurious bedroom. The king-size bed was magnificently covered in a beautiful ice-blue comforter, embroidered in a floral brown motif. On top, there were tons of coordinating pillows; it looked so inviting.

As I walked toward the bed, my dress was replaced with the cutest blue-and-brown pajama set. Of course, it matched perfectly with the bedding; I was nothing if not coordinated. I pulled the covers back and hopped in; Mokie followed suit. As I adjusted my body as I normally would, a comforting sigh escaped my lips as I closed my eyes. A few minutes into the effort, I spoke my thoughts into the air. "I will never fall asleep here, will I?"

"No," Ehren responded as he appeared and sat next to me on the bed. "There will never be a need to. Nothing you ever do here will exhaust or tire you."

Pondering Ehren's response made me smile. I would never tire here no matter what I did. I would never feel pain or be harmed. The realization of this place, its inhabitants, and its miracles was overwhelming. I was captivated by its workings, by its truths.

"You do look cute in your PJs though," my large friend said.

"Thanks," I responded with a toothy grin.

"You know she will be arriving soon. You'd better get to the corridor."

"I know," I said. "I'm so excited."

I stood at the doors of the corridor to wait for her arrival. Never did I imagine that I'd be welcoming her home. I was so honored to stand where my grandfather did as I arrived. I remembered the experience fondly. I began to hear footsteps in the distance. She was here.

As Cynthia approached me, her expression looked much like mine did when I saw my grandfather. She was as overwhelmed to see me as I was to see her. I opened my arms to take her in, and she melted into me. All her questions were answered about what happened to her friend, and she could see that I was just fine. The walls and doors of the corridor faded away to reveal the heaven she always knew existed. Cynthia's face lit up like a child's at Christmastime, and she could see everything God had promised. I was excited by the things she would see and do. Just then, she fell to her knees, put her head in her hands, and cried like a baby. As I watched my friend, now in a ball on the grass, they appeared and gathered around her much like they did with me in my kitchen at the château. I could see the interaction, and it was as if it were happening all over for me. I could feel the love they encircled my friend with. I began to walk away and let her experience everything the Father had for her, but I was stopped by the Father's hand on my shoulder.

"Stay," Jesus said with a smile.

While I stood still, the Father took Cynthia's hands in his, lifted her from the grass, and she looked upon his face for the first time. I never imagined that I could be included in a heavenly hug that was not my own. Being here with the Trinity and my best friend of almost forty years was glorious.

After the hug, I was left alone with the breeze on my fingertips, thinking of my friend and questioning, "Were Cynthia and I still best friends?" *No*, I thought, *because we are all the same in this place.*

"Not all of us," Ehren answered.

"What do you mean?" I asked.

"Well, *we* are not the same." He motioned to include the two of us in his "we." "I am very different from you and those like you. I was created as an angel, and you were created human. Humans will not become angels when they leave their planet and return home. Nor will they become a plant or a bird or a fish. They will always exist, but always in their original design. In answer to your question, you and Cynthia have always been together, and you always will be."

"What do you mean? I inquired.

"You don't remember anything prior to the life you've just lived, but you will. Haven't you ever felt like you've known someone forever?"

"Well, yeah," I said.

"That's because you have." Ehren went on, "Every human has what are called soul partners. Soul partners are those that will always be a part of your existence. Cynthia has always been with you because she, like many others, is one of your soul partners. You may not always know her in your existence as your best friend, but she will be close to you in one way or another."

"Are you saying that Cynthia could one day be my...mother?" I asked.

"No, little one." He tussled my hair. "After the thousand-year reign, when it is time, you will choose your parents, the continent on which you are born, and even your race according to the lessons you want to learn. When you have made that choice, it will begin for you and for your soul partners."

As we walked, my large friend almost had me until his last statement. I had to stop in my tracks and ask several questions. "Are you saying that when I make those choices as you just mentioned, Cynthia has to just go with me? She has to drop her heart's desire to tag along with me? How is that fair? How is that right?"

I couldn't help but feel outraged, and in heaven, that can't be a good thing. Ehren turned toward me, and seeing the state I had gotten myself into, he knelt so that we were face-to-face. "Tracy, the soul partners are as much a part of you as you are of them. You do not take the soul partners away from where they want to be. Their plans are made as yours are, and everything fits perfectly according to God's will. Do not fret. All is well."

I was still learning this place, and Ehren was such a blessing. I prayed for him as we continued to walk, and he thanked me. I still had questions about the soul partners, but I knew they would be answered here. I had questions about the whole going back to earth and learning new lessons. I knew that God's ways were not our ways. I just couldn't understand why I would ever want to leave what I have with him in this place. I walked home thinking of him and his greatness.

At the Schoolhouse

As I sat on the steps of the château, watching the colors of the heavenly sky begin to change and dissipate, a small schoolhouse appeared before me. The setting was rural, and the sky was blue, dotted with crisp white clouds. The clang of the school bell fixed my attention toward the red doors. The center split of the doors opened and spewed out its cargo. A dozen or so laughing and fast-moving children ran down the steps and into the play yard for recess. The children's clothing had seen better days, and their footwear left much to be desired. Some wore shoes that had clearly been outgrown; others were too big, and still others had none.

I moved toward the open doors. There was a nice, warm breeze; I could feel it blowing through my hair. I looked toward the front of the one-room schoolhouse to find Callie Mason. I, of course, had never met her, but I knew her in that instant. She was a dedicated and hardworking teacher. As I looked closer, I noticed that she wept.

"She weeps for the loss of her father, Jacob," the Holy Spirit spoke.

"I can feel her sorrow," I replied.

Pastor Jacob Mason had started the Mason School when he could find no one to teach his only daughter. He knew that an educated black could go further than an uneducated one, even if it wasn't but a little further; that's where he wanted Callie. The scenes of Jacob starting the school and all the ensuing struggles flew by in a blur. The severe beating he incurred prior to the last floorboard being placed did not stop him from being there to open the doors on the first day of classes. He stood so proud and grateful for God's protection that he dedicated the Mason School to the Father of all as he stood in the midst of all the citizens of his small black town.

"She remembers that day and how happy her father was," the Holy Spirit stated.

"What happened to her father? Did he die suddenly?" I inquired, fully expecting the Holy Spirit to reply.

"I was murdered." The response of Jacob Mason was crystal clear as he appeared next to me. Jacob went on to explain the troubles he incurred while he attempted to open his little schoolhouse. First, it was burned to the ground before it was even half finished; windows were smashed, and cow's blood and feces were smeared on its walls. The more traumas befell him, the more Jacob stood. He was determined that black children would learn to read and to write. I could see the images play out before me as he spoke. I could see and feel his determination to get the project done.

The schoolhouse was open less than a year before Jacob's death; his death, I discovered, was not why I was here at this moment watching his life unfold. I was here for Callie's journey. I watched as she shed her tears for her father, and I knew somehow that God had special plans for those little drops of pain. Callie was raised to be strong, and as the pictures flew by, I saw her struggles too. It was when her hair had turned gray and age had shown on her face that I could see Callie in the crowd as three of her students received their college diplomas. I could see why the Holy Spirit brought me the images. It was through Jacob's struggles that Callie found her place, and through Callie, the three college graduates found theirs.

"It has always been my plan that the people teach and raise up the other," the Holy Spirit declared.

"No one is meant to be alone to suffer. You are all one, and people are to learn from the past triumphs and adversities of others."

The Holy Spirit left me with that thought, and I proceeded to the chaise on my front porch to ponder it. Our ancestors paved the way for us through heartache, trials, laughter, and love. Times could be tough, but if we would slow down and learn the lessons of the past, we could create brighter futures. As I lay back on the cozy chaise, it opened itself to me and encased me. While I laid in its comfort, I began to remember my life. I remembered my mother, how beautiful she was, and how we laughed together. I remembered all the Sundays she'd take my sisters and me to the movies and to dinner. The consistency of that was so special. It was nice to have those memories flood my mind. It was nice to know I could recall them anytime I wanted.

I wanted to know everything about God, this place, and its workings. I stood and walked toward my angels as Mokie led the way. Merkin and Chezen stood tall and strong as they always had; I was happy to commune with them. I could feel their spirit as I stood between them. They were filled with God's pure love; their countenances were gentle and kind. They both looked down upon me and smiled. I could tell they were happy and content to be exactly where they were: here, with me.

My angels blessed me as Mokie and I walked down the steps and onto the street. We walked a bit and came upon Rosa Parks and Coretta Scott King. Rosa reached down to stroke Mokie's silky fur. The two proceeded to talk about the topic taught in the disciples' class, "God's creative ways." It sounded interesting, but after a brief exchange, I felt the need to move on. I would attend the class myself; I was sure of it.

"I want to know everything," I said to James as he appeared and began to walk with me.

"I felt that way too," he returned. "It's all so miraculous. I just wanted to see it all, do it all, and understand it all at the same time," he stated as he walked with me a little farther. James spoke of the wondrous things, people, and experiences he had been exposed to in this place.

The fact that heaven is created by the hearts' desires of its people was one of its most amazing qualities. I walked on as James left my presence, and I lifted my hands. The gentle, warm breeze caressed my fingertips, and it was like running my fingers through the spirit of God. Nothing but love, joy, peace, and creation could be felt. I was in heaven, in love, and in God's grace.

I found myself back in the château with Mokie by my side. I looked down to find myself clothed in a safari outfit, complete with hat, khaki shorts and shirt, knee socks, boots—the works. Surprisingly, I found slung across my body an elephant gun—a big one at that. I didn't have any history with guns or hunting, so this was a new one on me. I was in heaven, so what I would be doing with this gun was a mystery, but a mystery I was eager to explore. I walked down the stairs and out the front door to find my way to my next heavenly adventure. I figured that if I just started to walk, it would just happen. Walking farther, a lush jungle appeared all around me. I heard monkeys, birds, and sounds of the jungle. I was excited. As I walked on, I came upon a gathering of animals of all kinds. Lions, zebras, elephants, and giraffes mingled with cats, dogs, and hamsters. Walking closer, I could hear that the animals were all speaking to one another in their own voices. The lions roared, the dogs barked, and the elephants blew their trunks. They were all happy to share this space together.

The animals spoke of their adventures in heaven; some had been here since the beginning, and others had just arrived. As I continued to watch, a familiar face stood out; it was Mokie. Watching her with Bertram, the African elephant, and listening to their conversation filled me with joy. I was still amazed that not only could I hear the conversation taking place fifty feet away but I could totally understand the dialogue. I giggled as Mokie recanted her time in Paris.

As I leaned back against the hill that had appeared to support me, the Father appeared and sat next to me.

"So what do you think?" he asked.

"It's one of the most brilliant things I have ever seen," I responded. I turned to find the Father wearing a big smile. He was understandably pleased with what we both beheld. This place, this time was magical, and all of heaven's inhabitants knew it. I couldn't help but ask my Father a question.

"Father," I asked, "what's with the elephant gun?"

"I just thought it looked cool with the outfit," he said.

I couldn't help but giggle at his response. We turned our attention back to the animals.

"I have always loved animals," the Father said as we stood and began to walk toward the peacock and the tiger. Walking toward the animals, I noticed that they all began to bow. Every one of them, one after the other, purposed themselves to get low before Almighty God. It was all so beautiful. "They have always done this for me," he said. "They have had no barriers, no pride. They have always bowed before me." God shared with me without speaking a word that all animals bowed in his presence, in heaven and on earth.

After sharing a lovely time with my God and the animals, I found myself walking on a beautiful white sand beach, with the water lapping at my feet. Cynthia stood next to me. A white linen sundress replaced my safari getup.

"Wow," Cynthia said as we looked out over the water.

"I know," I added.

We faced each other on the shore and took each other in fully. It had been seven years since my death, and my friend had missed me terribly. The lack of our constant support of each other left a void in my friend's life. Losing her mother two years before my death was almost crippling to one of the strongest women I ever knew. Because of her kids, she kept moving on until she appeared in the corridor.

"I've missed you so much," she said.

"I know."

Cynthia and I walked arm in arm down the beach, with Ehren and Manoy close behind. I noticed in the distance a bluff that was the perfect place for Cynthia and me to share some time. Although the bluff ahead of us was at least one hundred feet up, Cynthia and I both took one step up, and we were there, seated in Adirondack chairs. I was so happy to share this special time with my friend. We talked and laughed for what seemed like hours.

I asked my friend what she'd like to do in the very next moment, and before she could answer, a table appeared before us. Upon the table was a vast array of entrées, desserts, fruit and cheese trays, and breads of all kinds. I remembered that food was a desire of Cynthia's heart even on earth. While being slender, Cynthia could always "put it away." I looked down to find a plate of grilled catfish. While I knew on earth that the catfish was the scavenger and considered dirty, I knew these catfish were pristine and I was about to get my grub on. Cynthia started with a perfect cut of prime rib with a baked potato, broccoli rice casserole, and a cup of clam chowder.

As we began to eat, the Trinity arrived, and each took a seat around the table. Here in this place were Cynthia's favorites: the Trinity, food, and me. We all talked, laughed, and ate everything that appeared before us. All that I saw before me was a desire of my friend's heart. I was so happy that she was here and happy and in the presence of God. As we finished up, the Father, Son, and Holy Ghost walked off the bluff and into the clouds.

Cynthia and I held each other again before she headed off to the clearing with Manoy to begin her training. I couldn't do anything but smile from ear to ear as my friend left. I was so happy to have her here and to know that she would be experiencing all the miraculous things of God. Mokie and I walked toward the gates and the clearing where the disciples were setting up. As we walked, I noticed a large pool of water. It was narrow, and it seemed to go on for miles and miles. This water was different; it was iridescent, and it sparkled. The water looked to be continuously filling the pool.

"They are the tears of God's people," Ehren said as he arrived.

"What do you mean?" I had to ask.

"Here is where God stores the tears of his people. Everything about your existence is important to him. Your tears, your breath, your…everything is here in this place, saved by the Father."

I looked again at the gathering of tears and was so moved. It was so beautiful. Ehren went on to tell me that the tears and the breath expelled by God's people would be returned to them and that what was expelled in pain, exasperation, and fatigue would be given back in strength and knowledge and love. I didn't know how God was going to do it, but I knew it would be mind-blowing.

I felt so blessed to have Ehren enlighten me on so many things; he was wonderful to have around. Walking and talking with him, I felt so connected to him, to this place, and to its inhabitants.

CHAPTER 17

And We Walked Together

I realized as I continued to walk that God *is* creation itself. He has been creating from the beginning. Since he uttered "Let there be light," creation has continued. Since we are all particles of God, it was always meant for us to continue to create. Creation is what God truly is about. Yes, God is love, but he is also creation. I sat down to ponder the thought.

As I began to recline, I felt my head and shoulders being supported—not by a small hill jutting up from the grass to meet me, but by Ehren. He lay behind me in the grass so that I was supported by his torso; if I looked to my left, I could see his face, or to the right, his massive legs and feet. There on the grass supported by my friend, I could hear the ocean.

"Are we near an ocean?" I asked.

"No," Ehren replied.

"So, why am I hearing crashing waves?" I inquired further.

"Because you love the sound," my friend responded.

"Is that coming from you?" I turned to look at his face.

"Yes."

"And the smell of coffee, is that you as well?"

"Yes. I can produce the smell of roses, pine needles, chocolate chip cookies, or anything else if you'd prefer."

"No," I said. "It's lovely…and so cool."

"I know," Ehren said with the enthusiasm of a child.

Lying in the grass with my friend, I could see the colors begin to form in the sky. I saw so many things burst into creation like the explosions made by fireworks on the Fourth of July, all whilst hearing the ocean in the background. Visions of the inventor and his or her invention sprang forth. I saw Da Vinci creating the *Mona Lisa* with his paintbrush. Choreographers and their creations danced across the sky; it was so exciting. I saw the Wright brothers as the initial thought of a flying machine was formed in their minds. So many incredible creations burst onto the screen of the sky. I watched George Washington Carver as he pondered what he was going to do with that peanut. I saw Bob Fosse, Alvin Ailey, J-Lo and Carrie Underwood as they created huge fantastic shows in their minds and then brought them to the stage for others to enjoy. I saw all these things as God himself saw them. It was the creative process that thrilled him. Never are we closer to him than when we create; I could see that, lying here with my friend. I sat up as the colors faded, and Ehren and I began to talk.

He affirmed everything I was thinking and saying. God loves us all, but he moves in *creation*. Faith is the beginning of creation; knowing that it can and will come into being brings it into being by our hand, by what we do. God wants us all to be prosperous as he is. If he thought living in shacks on dirt roads was the greatest thing, wouldn't heaven be made up of the same? God walks on streets of gold, and as we are his children, he wants the equal for us.

"Would you live happily in an opulent mansion and want Brittney to live in a hut made of twigs and vines? Of course, you wouldn't. It is the same for the Father toward his children," Ehren added.

My eyes were still being opened to the things of God as I walked with my friend in the grass of this wondrous place. I am spellbound that not only do I live here but, in my residency, God graciously gives me the knowledge of what he has created here.

"He really is remarkable," I said.

"I know," Ehren agreed.

Walking farther with Ehren, I began to feel excitement and enthusiasm. I didn't know why, but I knew that I would have my answer soon. As we walked, I looked to my left and to my right. People began to appear, and the ground beneath me began to rumble. I could do nothing but giggle and delight in all those who arrived. Christopher, Bum, and Cynthia were there. Mokie; Bertrand, the elephant; the Trinity; JonBenét; and Diana, the Princess of Wales, all stood with me for whatever was to come. They all seemed to know what was going on but left it as a surprise. Whatever was taking place was taking place for me.

As I stood in the miraculous rumble, up from the grounds of heaven sprang the biggest, most fantastic amusement park I had ever seen. Roller coasters, stage shows, arcades, bumper cars—anything my mind could fathom was there for our enjoyment, and boy, did we enjoy. We all ran toward the attractions like children. We were giddy and happy and over the moon. Christopher and I headed for the biggest, fastest roller coaster. There were twists and turns, a cork-screw, and even a water feature. I couldn't wait to get in it and go. We stepped to the front of the car and got in. I almost reached for the safety strap, but *Why?* was my thought. The coaster headed up and up and up and then banked to the right before plummeting back down with increasing speed. I couldn't hold it in, and I let out the biggest burst of laughter; I think the sound of it exploded through-out heaven. Christopher and I held up our hands and clapped and screamed and enjoyed every moment of the ride.

Afterward, Christopher headed to the bumper cars, and I joined Cynthia and Diana on the carousel. The horses tethered to it were alive and winged, as were the camels, zebras, lions, and giraffes. After choosing the zebra, JonBenét appeared and asked if she could ride with me, and of course, I agreed. As the music began to play and the ride began to turn, the animals began to exit the carousel plat-form and take their riders through the heavens of this glorious place. The music selection could still be heard emanating from the animals themselves. As we circled heaven, God, the Father, rode up next to me.

"Happy?" he asked as he smiled at me.

"Overjoyed!" was my reply. The group of riders rode through-out heaven, through the hills and valleys, and through fluffy white clouds and sparkling rainbows. The breeze, the smell of the air, and the music of praise that could be heard all around added to the delight of the ride. I noticed the animals began to gather together as we approached an archway; Cynthia, Diana, JonBenét, and I giggled like schoolgirls at recess. I looked ahead through the archway to see the same beautiful clouds we had been enjoying, but to my surprise, once we had crossed through the archway, the sky not only became black but filled with stars. My mouth hung open as I was riding a zebra in deep space, with Saturn no more than a mile away from me. I had seen some amazing things since my arrival, but this was more than miraculous. We all rode past planets we were familiar with and through galaxies we never knew existed. Millions of stars lay ahead of us, and they were all different in shape and size, much like snowflakes, only a gazillion times bigger. They were all so colorful, iridescent, and amazing. Some you could just put your hand through as if they were made of nothing at all.

I looked out onto what I was seeing and could not help but put my face in my hands and weep. It was all so beautiful, and I was in the middle of it with my God and those I had loved and lost. I could not hold on to what I was feeling here riding a zebra in space, and all I could do was cry. As I held my face in my hands, I felt her arrive.

"Why do you cry, my child?" the Holy Spirit spoke.

I looked up to respond, only to find that I was no longer atop my zebra with JonBenét but in her arms as I was with Jesus on the field in the coliseum.

"I am just so full and feel so blessed to be in this place, being a part of all this," I spoke through my tears.

"Tracy, this is your home. It always has been. You've just been away, but it will all come back to you. But I do love that you love it."

The Holy Spirit let me lie in her arms, in her comfort for some time, after which I was back on my zebra with JonBenét heading back to the carousel with the group. No earthly amusement park could come close to what I had just enjoyed. This one could only be designed by God himself, and I was so honored to have it spring to life just for me.

And We Walked Together

After the amusement park, I decided to head back to the château, but as I walked, nothing seemed familiar; however, I felt compelled to continue on. As I continued, I was joined by the Trinity. The Father walked on my left, Jesus to my right, and the Holy Spirit walked before us. I felt warm and comforted just as I did when they all appeared before me in my kitchen and gave the best hug I'd ever received. The scenery surrounding us was magnificent. We walked through a lush botanical garden. There were pathways and stone benches. I saw beautiful, mature trees. Oak, maple, and pine trees stood as far as the eye could see. Some were enormous. There were incredible flowers and plantings. There were hyacinths, lilies, and roses; wildflowers bloomed everywhere, and their aroma filled the air.

As we began to walk on, they all spoke to me simultaneously. They each nourished my soul and explained universal mysteries. The Father spoke specifically about life. He told how he created man from himself not only so that we, as individuals, could learn the lessons of the universe but so that he could experience those lessons in the physical through all of us. He spoke of being able to actually touch and feel through us. He reminded me that he is a spirit being and that to touch the physical, he had to become physical. He let me know that Jesus, in spite of contrary belief, was not the first one with whom he experienced the physical; Adam was.

"I could inhabit Adam and touch through his flesh, breathe through his lungs and nostrils. I could run with him and feel the power of the human body at work."

We spoke about man's ability to create his own existence—to become anything he wanted to become by simply thinking it; and by thinking it, feeling it, and applying it, he would create it.

Jesus continued and detailed the law of attraction and how man must seek out its benefits. "Study to show thyself approved" stirred in my mind as he spoke those words. "When the world was created, the laws of how to function in it were also created. I never intended it to be a secret," he stated. "The law was created so that man did not have to endure hardships in a world so abundant and so that he could concentrate on learning the many lessons the universe had to teach. The concept that opposites attract is false," he explained. "Like attracts like. When human beings think about how poor they are or how they don't make enough money, they will always be poor and not make enough money—because that's all they think about. It may not be what they want, but it is what they think about, and you bring about what you think about. Constant thoughts and feelings of abundance and wealth will bring about abundance and wealth because you will attract things into your life that, if applied correctly, will bring you abundance and wealth. My law of attraction was kept to the few who became wealthy and satisfied with their existence while the masses were poor, downtrodden, and persecuted. I have continued to inspire my people to look deeper into different concepts and to seek out more than just one source of my wisdom. I have detailed everything in so many of man's publications. If my people would but seek and listen to those I have given my voice to, they could all live in abundance. There is enough prosperity and abundance for everyone," he said as he handed me a fragrant white rose.

"If my children choose to live a life of illness, depression, and poverty, by reason of free will, it is their choice, and I cannot affect it. By the same token, if they choose a life of wealth, affluence, power, health, and well-being, I cannot affect those choices either, and they will thrive." The Holy Spirit spoke of the fruit of the spirit in great detail: love, joy, peace, longsuffering, gentleness, goodness, faith, meekness, and temperance. They were not just pleasant words but words that had power if only men would study their meanings and adjust their lives accordingly.

The ways of God are vast yet so simple, and the Father, Son, and Holy Spirit made sure I was aware of it. I was left alone with the Father, and we walked on a bit farther; I could tell there was more wisdom he wanted to impart.

"Tracy," he said, looking deep into my eyes.

"Yes, Father," I said.

"I want to give you the answer to an age-old question—a question that has plagued man for some time."

"Yes, Father. What is it?" I stood motionless as he began to speak.

"Why did the chicken cross the road?" he said.

I couldn't believe my ears. I was stunned and speechless, so he asked the question again.

"My child."

I knew he meant business when he used the phrase "my child," so needless to say, I knew this was going to be seriously *universal* and deep.

"Why did the chicken cross the road?" he repeated.

"I don't know, Father. Why?" I waited in anticipation and expectation of the godly wisdom.

"Because...I told it to!"

With that, the Father exploded in laughter. I couldn't believe it. He slapped his leg and could hardly get a breath. His laughter was infectious. Not only did I have to laugh, but so did the grass, flowers, and trees. As he left me, departing up through the canopy of trees, I could hear his laughter trailing behind him.

I walked through the beautiful garden for what seemed like hours and hours. This was surely the garden Christopher had spoken of earlier. As I walked, I felt the light, warmth, and peace of this place. I sat at the base of a magnificent tree. It stretched up strong and tall. Mokie joined me as I leaned back and closed my eyes. As I stroked her head, I remembered everything I'd experienced since my arrival. It all came back to me simultaneously; everything was so amazing. I thought how blessed we all truly are, to simply be a particle of him. He is so mind-blowing and utterly fantastic.

"I always knew this place was here, but there was just no way to fathom it in my mind while on earth," I said to Ehren as he appeared next to me under the tree.

"I know, but what you've seen is only the beginning. There is much more for you to see and to do."

I pondered Ehren's statement as we all walked toward the château. On the short journey home, I noticed everyone that I had encountered today. They were all there, still waving and welcoming me. Nothing but love filled the street. I was home where I belonged.

Christopher was here, and it was brilliant. My daughter, my best friend, Mokie, James, and Bum were all here. All those I thought I'd lost are found here in this place. This place, this heaven is here, and it's real, so real I can taste it and breathe it and create it. I have seen so many things I'd never dreamed of seeing, done so many things I'd never dreamed of doing. I had lunch in Paris with my dog and shopped with Brittney as she slept. How sweet, gracious, and wise the Father is to create and want to share this place with all of us. All the times I thought I was unworthy, I was wrong. All the times I thought I wasn't good enough, I was wrong. All the times I thought I'd never make it here, I was wrong.

My mansion, my dog, my piano, and my two angels were just waiting for me to arrive. As I began to walk in this place, it opened itself up to me and let me see it from the beginning. My mind was full of wonder and excitement. I was expectant to see what was next. I knew that I could sit here on my front porch and watch it all happen, or I could go out and create it with every step I took. I was in heaven; I was home.

Just then, the sky began to light up with colors.

Thank you for taking the time to read this book. If you, by chance, have not accepted Jesus Christ as your Lord and Savior but would like to, below you will find the Sinner's Prayer. Romans 3:23 states, "For all have sinned, and fallen short of the glory of God."

SINNER'S PRAYER

Father God,
I admit that I am a sinner, and I ask for your forgiveness.
I believe that Jesus Christ is the Son of God and that he died
and rose from the dead for my sins. I confess Jesus as my
Lord and Savior. I repent of my sins and surrender my life to you.
I pray this in Jesus's name. Amen.

If you prayed that prayer with a humble, sincere heart,
let me be the first to welcome you to the family.
Next step will be to find yourself a Bible-based church and learn
about the Father that loves you more than you know.

ABOUT THE AUTHOR

Tracy D. Palmer is an author living in Fort Worth, Texas. After being given the confirmed prophecy of "God told me to tell you, you are the writer of the vision," she put her faith in God and never looked back. Tracy enjoys travel, organizing, fashion, decorating, and spending time with family and friends, especially her granddaughter, Sofia.

CPSIA information can be obtained
at www.ICGtesting.com
Printed in the USA
BVHW071153240619
551796BV00004B/597/P